Spiritual
DISCERNMENT
and
THE MIND
of CHRIST

Spiritual DISCERNMENT *and* THE MIND *of* CHRIST

*Possessing the mind of the Redeemer
in an age of negativity and deceit*

FRANCIS FRANGIPANE

Spiritual Discernment and the Mind of Christ

Published by Arrow Publications, Inc.
P.O. Box 10102
Cedar Rapids, IA 52410

Teachings/Conferences: Frangipane.org
Ministry Resources/Books: Arrowbookstore.com

Printed in the United States of America

ISBN 978-1-886296-36-7

CONTENTS

* these chapters were adapted from previously published books

Introduction

Within the pages of this book we will discuss a number of ways spiritual discernment can mature in our lives. Certainly we need discernment. But for many, discernment exists on a primitive level – that is to say, whatever makes them angry is rendered "bad" and whatever makes them happy is discerned as "good."

We need a better source of discernment than our subjective feelings.

Thus, my observations will be built upon a number of supportive Scriptures. I firmly believe the Word of God, under the tutelage of the Holy Spirit, is our surest source of inspiration. It has been my practice to read a different translation of the Bible each year, as I have been able. At the same time, I certainly do not consider my interpretations or perceptions to be infallible; I'm sure others wiser than me will find legitimate opportunities to upgrade or expand my thinking about various topics. I welcome their input.

For now, I will build upon the foundation of God's Word. In all, I hope to present a balanced and healthy approach to this important study.

However, let me add another goal, a higher goal. I believe we can actually gain access to the mind of Christ. To facilitate this goal, I have not only provided new chapters, but I have included certain previously published teachings.

I admit there could be some redundancy in combining the new with the old. Please forgive this weakness. I've done this for the sake of those readers for whom the entire book will be new material. These classic chapters are foundational to our understanding of spiritual discernment. Indeed, they help give continuity and depth to our present discussion on this important subject.

Finally, dear friend, let us hold fast to God's hand of grace as we climb the mountain of His truth, and let us shelter ourselves in the peace of Christ. For our pursuit of discernment is not merely doctrinal or cerebral but relational. We are seeking to possess the mind and heart of Jesus Christ, the Redeemer of mankind.

Publisher's Note

The demand for information on spiritual discernment in general spurred the writing of this present work. Although a few of these chapters were borrowed from previously published books by Pastor Frangipane, all of them have been rewritten and updated.

Included with each previously published chapter you will find the source for that material should you desire more information on the subject. Please see the back pages for more on all our resources.

Our hope is to provide the most information to help the most people. In this effort, we recalled the Lord's encouraging words to the scribes of the kingdom – that we too would bring "out of [our] treasure things new and old" (Matt. 13:52).

—Arrow Publications, Inc.

PART ONE

THE MIND
OF CHRIST

The core work of our destiny
is conformity to Jesus Christ.
Thus, we must learn to view life
not with the graceless mind of a faultfinder
but with the compassionate mind
of the Redeemer.

Let this mind be in you
which was also in Christ Jesus.

— PHILIPPIANS 2:5 NKJV —

1

A SOCIETY OF REDEEMERS

Before we discuss a number of ways we can develop our powers of discernment, let us acknowledge that our world is under a great, multidimensional assault. Hell is advancing and its goal is to swallow civilizations in darkness. I've seen the demonic legions, strident in their rebellion, shaking their fists toward Heaven as they lay claim to our open and foolishly naive cultures.

I have even known, on occasion, the intimidation of the Prince of Darkness. I've felt the weight of his confidence as he gloats at how unprepared the church is – how divided and carnal. He has no doubt that ultimately his kingdom will completely rule this world.

However, Jesus declared plainly that, "Scripture cannot be broken" (John 10:35). No word spoken by

God can return to Him void; every word spoken by the Almighty will accomplish its divinely appointed purpose (Isa. 55:11). Thus, the immutable Word declares it will be the kingdom of the Most High that expands worldwide, not the kingdom of darkness. As it is written of God's kingdom, "There will be no end to [its] increase" (Isa. 9:7).

Again, God's Word says that "in the last days the mountain of the house of the Lord will be established as the chief of the mountains ... and all the nations will stream to it" (Isa. 2:2). Yes, even as I see darkness spreading, advancing and covering the earth, and deep darkness covering the people, I remain encouraged. For it is in this very context that the Spirit assures us: "But the Lord will rise upon you and His glory will appear upon you" (Isa. 60:2). As a result, the Most High pledges that "nations will come to your light, and kings to the brightness of your rising!" (Isa. 60:3).

And yes, we know the world will enter the period of the Antichrist, the Rapture and the tribulation. Yet rage as he will, even Satan will ultimately realize his defeat. The prince of darkness will bow his knee and with his tongue acknowledge that "Jesus Christ is Lord, to the glory of God the Father" (Phil. 2:10–11; Rom. 14:11).

Therefore let us not surrender to fear or unbelief. If Satan has legions of demons, God has an army of redeemers. In truth, as each of us matures, we must stop thinking of ourselves merely as "church people" and more as a society of redeemers, for that is what we become as we are conformed to the heart of Jesus Christ (Rom. 8:28–29).

Transforming Our Anger

Yes, there are times when I feel completely outraged by what the devil is doing to people, especially children. I burn inwardly with anger at the injustice and heartache I see in the world. But I know that my anger, by itself, cannot attain the righteousness of God (James 1:20). I must gather my passions and submit them to the Holy Spirit that they may regenerate into a redemptive response, even one that empowers my conformity to Christ.

I know many believe redemption on a citywide or larger scale is not possible in our day – that all that awaits us is the Rapture. Let us not minimize the great hope promised by God in the rapture of the church! If the Rapture happens today, I will certainly be prepared. But what if it does not occur for another twenty years or more? I don't want to be found looking up at the skies when there remains a great work to be done on earth.

Therefore, let's arm ourselves with discernment and wisdom, and reach in faith to possess the mind of Christ. Jesus said, "This gospel of the kingdom shall be preached in the whole world as a testimony to all the nations, and then the end will come" (Matt. 24:14). The world has seen Christianity; let us now reveal Christ as He manifests Himself through a society of redeemers.

2

BECAUSE HE LIVES IN US

It is time to redefine ourselves. As stated in chapter one, no more should we think of ourselves only as traditional Christians. Let us, instead, see ourselves as a society of redeemers. As we learn to think as a redeemer, we will increasingly find our thoughts being synchronized with the mind of Christ.

One may argue that no mere man or woman who has been a sinner can become a redeemer. I agree, we cannot pay the full price for someone's redemption. To think otherwise is blaspheme. At the same time, there is not a different Jesus in us than mankind's Redeemer who ascended into Heaven; Christ is the Redeemer seated in Heaven and He is the Redeemer seated in us.

You see, at some point, Christ will no longer be to you just a doctrine or a religion. Through the Holy

Spirit, He will begin to reveal Himself in tangible ways. As a result, you will increasingly become "radioactive" with His actual presence.

If we are true sheep, we will begin to discern His voice. We will see evidences of His protection and healing that we never recognized before. Just as we become holy because He is holy (1 Pet 1:16), so we become redeemers because He is the Redeemer.

As it is written, "As He is, so also are we in this world" (1 John 4:17).

Therefore, let me assure you that if we walk with Him we will inevitably think like Him. His influence, like leaven, will spread throughout our thoughts and into our very motives. His prayer life will increasingly influence our prayers. His promises will strengthen us when we are weak. Just as He promised, "The one who says he abides in Him ought himself to walk in the same manner as He walked" (1 John 2:6).

NEARNESS TO CHRIST

You see, it is our nearness to Christ that produces virtue, healing gifts and spiritual discernment. As Jesus promised: "He who believes in Me, the works that I do, he will do also" (John 14:12).

We generally assume the Lord was referring to miracles when He said we would accomplish the works that He did. However, while miracles are part of the overall works of Christ, Jesus did not limit His definition of "works" to the miraculous. The works He did were diverse and many: He lived a redemptive life; He spent nights in prayer; He forgave His persecutors; He identified with the poor and needy; He rendered Himself as a guilt offering for mankind's sins, and so on. If Christ truly becomes our life, then *all* the works that He did, we "will do also," and this includes what I refer to as possessing the mind of Christ.

Because He lives within us, we see that Isaiah 53 does not apply exclusively to Jesus; by extension, it also becomes the blueprint for Christ in us. Indeed, was this not part of His reward, that He would see His offspring (v.10)? True Christians are the progeny of Christ.

Listen to Paul's heart,

> *Now I rejoice in my sufferings for your sake, and in my flesh I do my share on behalf of His body, which is the church, in filling up what is lacking in Christ's afflictions.*
>
> —*Colossians 1:24*

What does the apostle mean? Did not Christ fully pay mankind's debts once and for all? Is he implying that we now take Jesus' place? No. We will never take Jesus' place. *It means that Jesus has come to take our place.*

19

Again, as Paul wrote,

> *I have been crucified with Christ; and it is no longer I who live, but Christ lives in me; and the life which I now live in the flesh I live by faith in the Son of God, who loved me and gave Himself up for me.*   —*Galatians 2:20*

This is how very close Christ is to us: *He is in our thoughts. He dwells in our hearts.* As far as God's view of us goes, it is no longer I who live, but Christ lives in me. What remains of my human nature lives by faith in the Son of God.

Why do we not perceive Him more clearly? Perhaps it is because we are out of sync with His motives. However, as we reach for conformity to Christ, our spirits begin to align with His. In time, as our powers of discerning His voice improve, we will better hear Him. By His grace, our abilities to distribute the blessings of Heaven to those around us will also improve. Christians are not just people who are going to Heaven; in real ways, are we not also people coming from Heaven – possessing the goods, power and virtue of Heaven?

What We Must Avoid

This reality – that we are influenced by the indwelling mind of Christ – creates in us the exact opposite attitude of the unbelieving, self-righteous Pharisees and scribes. Our quest is to be conformed to Jesus Christ, who reminds us to truly learn of Him, that He is meek and lowly of heart (Matt. 11:29). Jesus did not avoid the poor or sick; He was drawn to them. Compassion and humility are fundamental aspects of the mind of Christ.

As a society of redeemers, we must flee from loveless attitudes, especially the Pharisaic attitude of those who trust in themselves that they are righteous while viewing others with contempt (Luke 18:9–14).

My appeal in publishing this work is that, in spite of the conflicts in our world and regardless of the ever accelerating advance of hell, we do not abandon our role to serve God's redemptive purposes. Remember: "God ... always leads us in triumph in Christ, and manifests through us the sweet aroma of the knowledge of Him in every place" (2 Cor. 2:14). May the world see Jesus manifest through us.

Concerning this vision of possessing Christ's likeness, I must admit there exists a certain degree of hypocrisy among us Christians. What I mean is, without qualms we condemn the world for not being Christian, yet without remorse we tolerate that we are not Christlike.

I am not saying we shouldn't cry out against evil. However, at some point we must recognize there is more to our destiny than judging sin in other people. God is looking for the perfection of mercy within us; "mercy triumphs over judgment" (James 2:13).

Recall the words of Paul: "Let this mind be in you, which was also in Christ Jesus" (Phil. 2:5 KJV). He goes on to explain that Christ existed in the form of God, yet He emptied Himself, took the form of a man, and died for our sins. In other words, He saw mankind's sin and need, but instead of condemning humanity, He died on our behalf. Paul says we are to have this same attitude in us.

Perhaps we cannot imagine, based on our current level of growth, what it means to attain "the stature which belongs to the fullness of Christ" (Eph. 4:13). Yet we can take the next steps. We can press on toward that lofty goal. What we do know is this: as the Father sent Jesus, so Jesus now sends us (John 20:21).

In following Him, and through our union with Him, we become a fellowship of deliverers. Obadiah 1:21 says,

> *The deliverers will ascend Mount Zion*
> *To judge the mountain of Esau,*
> *And the kingdom will be the Lord's.*

We are not deliverers in the way Jesus delivered the world, but within the sphere of our limited environment – in our world of friends, family and community – we exercise the same mentality as Christ: *we seek not to judge our world but to save it.*

Of course, along the way the enemy will seek to stop us. He will use offenses, slander and persecution. However, as Christ followers, when wounded, we forgive; when forced to go one mile, we go two. We bless those who curse us and turn the other cheek to those who strike us.

Just as Christ hung on the cross at Calvary and prayed, "Father, forgive them" (Luke 23:34), so we too stand in prayer before God on behalf of our communities and, at times, even our enemies. Like Christ, His apostles, and millions of other true followers of mankind's Redeemer, we pray the mercy prayer. We do so because He lives in us. In light of the increasing warfare in our world, it is a most profound truth: we can actually possess the thinking processes of Jesus. Indeed, spiritual discernment is the by-product of possessing the mind of Christ.

3

WHAT DOES JESUS SAY?

GREAT GAIN

We must relearn how to think. We must learn how to pause before we speak – give ourselves a moment to enter the secret place of God's presence – and then listen to what Jesus has to say. For Christ Himself is the source of our discernment. In listening, we create the opportunity to hear the Lord's voice; postured before Him we can receive answers, wisdom and insights that we otherwise would not discern.

Indeed, using the gift of discernment, we can counter the advance of the enemy and reverse the gains he might have otherwise obtained. Consider the gospel story of the woman caught in the act of adultery (John 8:1–11). As experts in the Mosaic Law, the Pharisees knew well that the woman sinned. Wishing to publicly discredit

Jesus, they brought her to Him hoping, perhaps, to prove Him a heretic:

> *"Teacher, this woman has been caught in adultery, in the very act. Now in the Law Moses commanded us to stone such women; what then do You say?"*   *—John 8:4–5*

This is the big question: *What does Jesus say?* Everything we will learn about discernment is found in knowing the answer to this question. There will be pressure to answer. It's likely that turmoil may surround us. Yet we must stay sheltered in the calm of God. The woman is obviously guilty; witnesses have condemned her, as does the Law of Moses. Stones are waiting in the hands of her accusers. But if we will actually possess true discernment we must stop, listen, and actually hear: *What does Jesus say?*

Christ recognizes her sin. However, His thoughts were higher than that of the Pharisees. He saw this situation as a means to bring redemption to the woman, repentance to the Pharisees, and glory to His heavenly Father. Stooping down, He wrote on the ground. Then, as the Pharisees persisted with their accusations, He stood and said, "He who is without sin … let him be the first to throw a stone" (John 8:7).

The hardened hearts of the Pharisees were so deeply pierced that, "one by one, beginning with the older ones," they departed (v. 9). Scripture does not tell us what Jesus wrote (some say He wrote one of the Ten Commandments or perhaps some other Scripture). What He wrote is unknown. However, in the Lord's response He made it clear: in His kingdom, the merciful and the pure in heart decide when, and if, stones will be thrown.

The issue I seek to underscore is not that Jesus drew on the ground but that, in the heightened turmoil of the moment, Jesus drew upon the Father. He remained calm. He waited, listening in His heart to hear the voice of His Father.

This is the pattern for true discernment: we disown the limits of our opinions and reactions, and we learn to wait and listen to the Lord.

AS THE VOICE COMES TO ME

Jesus expands this discipline of focused waiting. Consider His comment in John 5:

> *I am able to do nothing from Myself [independently, of My own accord – but only as I am taught by God and as I get His orders]. Even as I hear, I judge [I decide as I am bidden to decide. As the voice comes to Me, so I give a decision].* —John 5:30 AMP

Jesus said, "As the voice comes to Me, so I give a decision." This small statement unveils such a large truth!

When we accept Christ into our hearts, He does not enter simply as a doctrine. No, He enters us as a living voice. His Spirit brings conviction and direction; He speaks through dreams, visions, revelation, and understanding of the Scriptures. He illuminates our hearts, speaking to us of repentance and the renewal of our soul. He lifts us, reminding us of the faithful promises of God.

Yet this voice – the sacred voice of God – refuses to compete with the clamor of our fleshly minds. This is God, King and Creator of the universe. He requires the honor of our full attention! He will not yell as though we were disobedient children and He a frantic mother. He will not chase us. He waits.

Yes, there are times when He may resist us, gently pushing against our prideful efforts. He will wait until we stop our harmful activity. Our problem is not that God won't come to us; it's that our anxious souls fail to give Him time to speak.

Remember, His thoughts are "higher than" our thoughts (Isa. 55:9). He would speak to us, but our opinions monopolize the conversation. Our ideas and preprogrammed reactions rush out of our mouths and into the world of men. We hurry by the narrow path that leads to His presence. He is left out of the conversation; He wants in.

Jesus taught, "Take care what you listen to" (Mark 4:24). Do we truly know how to listen? Discernment is the art of listening to Him who does not speak audibly and perceiving Him who is otherwise invisible. And the one great question that leads to all we need to know is this: *What does Jesus say?*

4

THE GIFT OF
DISCERNMENT

If we will serve with true discernment, our perception must be renewed until we see life through the eyes of Christ the Redeemer.

TO DISCERN, YOU CANNOT JUDGE

We will never possess mature, ongoing discernment until we crucify our instincts to judge. Realistically, for most of us, this may take an extended, focused season of uprooting old thought-systems – attitudes that were not planted in faith and love for people. In truth, if we will appropriate the discernment born in the "mind of Christ," we must first find the heart of Christ (1 Cor. 2:16). The heart and love of Jesus is summed up in His own words: "I did not come to judge the world, but to save the world" (John 12:47). Yet even when the Lord does judge us, it is to save and deliver us.

Spiritual discernment is the grace to see into the unseen. It is a gift of the Spirit to perceive the realm of the spirit. Its purpose is to understand the nature of that which is veiled. However, the first veil that must be removed is the veil over our own hearts. For the capacity to see into that which is in another's heart comes from Christ revealing that which is in our own hearts. Before He reveals the sin of another, the Lord requires we grasp our own deep need of His mercy. Thus, out of the grace that we have received, we can compassionately minister grace to others. We will know thoroughly that the true gift of discernment is not a faculty of our minds.

Christ's goal is to save, not judge. Consider our task: We are called to navigate the narrow and well-hidden path into the true nature of men's needs. If we would truly help men, we must remember, we are following the Lamb.

This foundation must be laid correctly, for in order to discern, you cannot react. To perceive, you must make yourself blind to what seems apparent. People may react to you, but you cannot react to them. You must always remain forgiving in nature, for the demons you cast out will challenge you, masquerading as the voice of the person you seek to deliver. You must discern the difference between the oppressing spirit and the person oppressed.

Thus, Jesus prepared His disciples to be proactive in their forgiveness. Using Himself as their example, He taught, "Everyone who speaks a word against the Son of Man, it will be forgiven him" (Luke 12:10). Jesus prepared His heart to forgive men before they ever sinned against Him. He knew His mission was to die for men, not condemn them.

As His followers, we are called to carry the banner of His redemptive mission. In His prayer to the Father, Jesus said, "As You sent Me into the world, I also have sent them" (John 17:18). We are called to die that others may live. Therefore, we must realize that before our perception develops, our love must mature until our normal attitude is one of forgiveness. Should God call us to release men from spiritual bondage, we cannot react to the confrontational things they may say. As our perception becomes more like Christ Himself and the secrets of men's hearts are revealed, we cannot even react to what men think.

If we do not move in divine forgiveness, we will walk in much deception. We will presume we have discernment when, in truth, we are seeing through the veil of a critical spirit. We must know our weaknesses, for if we are blind to our sins, what we assume we discern in men will merely be the reflection of ourselves.

Indeed, if we do not move in love, we will actually become a menace to the body of Christ.

This is exactly what Jesus taught when He said,

> *"Do not judge so that you will not be judged. For in the way you judge, you will be judged; and by your standard of measure, it will be measured to you. Why do you look at the speck that is in your brother's eye, but do not notice the log that is in your own eye? Or how can you say to your brother, 'Let me take the speck out of your eye,' and behold, the log is in your own eye? You hypocrite, first take the log out of your own eye, and then you will see clearly to take the speck out of your brother's eye."*
>
> *—Matthew 7:1–5*

Repentance is the removal of the "logs" within our vision; it is the true beginning of seeing clearly. There are many who suppose they are receiving the Lord's discernment concerning one thing or another. Perhaps in some things they are; only God knows. But many are simply judging others and calling it discernment. Jesus commanded us to judge not. He sends us into the world not as judges of man but, under Him, as co-redeemers. We are not sent to condemn people but to rescue them. Thus, let us accept this season of crucifixion of our critical ways and condescending attitudes.

THE GOAL IS TO SEE CLEARLY

The judgmental carnal mind always sees the image of itself in others. Without realizing it is seeing itself, it assumes it is perceiving others. Jesus refers to the person who judges as a "hypocrite." The Lord is not saying we should totally stop thinking about people. He wants us to be able to help one another. The emphasis in Jesus' command to "not judge" is summarized in His concluding remark:

> *"First take the log out of your own eye, and then you will see clearly to take the speck out of your brother's eye."*   —*Matthew 7:5*

The way we help is not by judging but by seeing clearly. This is the "righteous judgment" of which Jesus speaks in John 7:24. We do not "see clearly" until we have been through deep and thorough repentance, until the instinct to judge after "appearances" is uprooted.

We have seen that Jesus paralleled speaking to people about their sins with taking specks out of their eyes. The eye is the most tender, most sensitive part of the human body. How do you take a speck out of someone's eye? Very carefully! First, you must win their trust. This means consistently demonstrating an attitude that does not judge, one that will not instinctively condemn. To help others, we must see clearly.

If you seek to have a heart that does not condemn, you must truly crucify your instinct to judge. Then you will have laid a true foundation for the gift of discernment, for you will have prepared your heart to receive dreams, visions and insights from God. You will be unstained by human bias and corruption.

—Adapted from *The Three Battlegrounds*

5

Eliminating False Discernment

There is a "jamming station" made up of our own thoughts and reactions that inhibits our powers of discernment. Until the motor of the carnal mind is turned off, true discernment will not consistently be ours. We must die to personal judgments, ideas of retaliation and self-motivation. Indeed, Jesus said, "I can do nothing on My own initiative. As I hear, I judge" (John 5:30). Inwardly Jesus ceased striving. We also must learn to listen to the voice of the Holy Spirit. As we stop our striving, as we hear God, we discern and judge rightly.

Abounding Love Brings Discernment with It

Paul wrote, "This I pray, that your love may abound still more and more in real knowledge and all discernment" (Phil. 1:9). Discernment comes from abounding love. What is abounding love? It is love that leaps out from us toward others. It is motivated by long-term commitment; it is anointed by sacrificial charity.

There is a false discernment that is based on mistrust, suspicion and fear. You can recognize false discernment by the coldness around it. False discernment may be packaged in a type of love, but it does not originate in love; it comes out of criticism. True discernment is rooted deeply in love.

Picture, if you will, a long-haired young man. His clothes are unkempt and he has tattoos on his arms. It is night and he is walking toward you on a lonely street. It is easy to judge such a person after the obvious and superficial. Now look at this young man in the same setting but as his mother would see him. You can still see his outer appearance, but when you look at him, you have insight into his life and hope for his future. You see a little boy growing up without a father, a child rejected often by his friends. You have a commitment toward this young man that runs deep. It has been sustained by the love you have carried since you suffered in giving him birth.

False discernment sees the outside of the person or situation and pretends it knows the inside. Godly discernment comes from having godly motives; godly motives are those rooted in God's committed love. In like manner, our capacity to discern the needs of the church will never rise higher than that which is superficial if we do not know Christ's heart for His people.

Jesus said, "Do not judge according to appearance, but judge with righteous judgment" (John 7:24). Righteous judgment is the direct result of love. If you cannot pray in love for a person or the church, do not presume you have true discernment. Love precedes peace, and peace precedes perception. Without love and peace in your heart, your judgment will be overly harsh. Regardless of the smile upon your face, your heart will have too much anger. False discernment is always slow to hear, quick to speak, and quick to anger.

PEACE MUST RULE OUR HEARTS

There is a tension underlying false discernment, an anxiety that pressures the mind to make a judgment. True discernment emerges out of a tranquil and pure heart, one that is almost surprised by the wisdom and grace in the voice of Christ. Remember, our thoughts will always be colored by the attitudes of our hearts. Jesus said, "The mouth speaks out of that which fills the heart" (Matt. 12:34). He also said, "Out of the heart of men, proceed the evil thoughts" (Mark 7:21). Again He said, "The pure in heart ... shall see God"

(Matt. 5:8). From the heart the mouth speaks, the eyes see, and the mind thinks. In fact, Proverbs 4:23 (NKJV) tells us to diligently guard our hearts, "for out of [the heart] spring the issues of life."

Life, as we perceive it, is based upon the condition of our heart. This is very important because the gifts of the Spirit must pass through our hearts before they are presented to the world around us. In other words, if our hearts are not right, the gifts will not be right either.

When the heart has unrest it cannot hear from God. Therefore, we must learn to mistrust our judgment when our heart is bitter, angry, ambitious or harboring strife for any reason. The Scriptures tell us to, "let the peace of Christ rule [act as arbiter] in [our] hearts" (Col. 3:15). To hear clearly from God, we must first have peace.

Solomon wrote, "One hand full of rest is better than two fists full of labor and striving after wind" (Eccl. 4:6). There is too much labor and toil in our minds, too much striving after the wind. If we want discernment we must become aggressively calm. This is not a passive state of mind but an expectant, focused waiting upon God. Discernment comes from our sensitivity to Christ in the realm of the Spirit. It comes as we allow love to be our motivation and secure the peace of Christ in our hearts. Through a life so prepared by God, the gift of discernment is revealed.

—Adapted from *The Three Battlegrounds*

6

LOVE JUST ONE

The moment we accept a biblical world view, our powers of discernment start to become active. For the most part, however, our spiritual faculties are still immature and undeveloped. Like a newborn, we see and hear, but it is difficult to bring things into focus. While we may have better clarity concerning good and evil, we usually do not know how to process what we see. We often find ourselves judging people rather than actually having revelatory insight into how to help them.

Yet the gifts of God are, in truth, living realities. As such, we should expect our powers of discernment to grow – and nothing accelerates that growth process like focusing our vision on conformity to Christ. The closer we come to abiding in Christ and His words, the more truly we can expect to understand how He thinks and what motivates His heart.

Many challenge the idea that, as mere humans, we can actually perceive the Lord's thoughts. We have too often heard those who proclaimed that "God told" them such and such when it wasn't true. Still, because others fail to hear clearly should that disqualify us from reaching for the potential stated in Scripture? Let not the failures of others stop our pursuit of Christ's likeness. Others argue, even using Scripture, "Who has known the mind of the Lord?" (1 Cor. 2:16).

Yes, certainly, the Lord has His pocket full of awesome surprises. I am not saying we can "figure out" all there is to the divine nature. I am stating only that we do not have to sleepwalk or float through life; we can be led by a true, living word from God that is directed personally to us.

Recall that Jesus told His disciples, "Blessed are your eyes, because they see; and your ears, because they hear" (Matt. 13:16). Our Lord assures us that those who follow Him shall also be trained by Him; as trained disciples, they would experience a level of blessedness that He Himself defined as having eyes that see and ears that hear. Our spiritual faculties can be enhanced and filled with the Holy Spirit. We absolutely can know the temperament of God, and as we grow we can learn the language of the Almighty.

THE UPWARD CALL

It is sad, but many Christians muddy along, hoping for nothing loftier than a short reprieve from sin, guilt and self-condemnation. Should the lowliness of our sinful state have veto power over the enormity of God's promises? May it never be! For Scripture assures us that our call, even as lowly as we feel sometimes, is an upward climb that relies upon faith in God's abilities and our Lord's redemption. We are not harnessed to our flaws and weaknesses; rather, in spirit-to-Spirit fusion we are united to the resurrection power of Heaven! Our call is not merely to attend church but to walk with God, whose eternal goal has predestined us to be "conformed to the image of His Son" (Rom. 8:29).

Yes, let us deeply repent for our sins and learn to walk humbly with our God, but let us not assume faith must depart so humility may arise. No, our adoption as sons and daughters has made us joint heirs with Christ. You see, everything concerning our salvation and the gifts of God in our lives comes to us not as something we attain by works but as an inheritance we receive by faith.

The Spirit Himself testifies with our spirit that we are children of God, and if children, heirs also, heirs of God and fellow heirs with Christ. —Romans 8:16–17

45

Therefore let us set our hopes high upon the promises of God. Though we fall, the Lord will lift us (Prov. 24:16; Micah 7:7–8). God's grace will not wilt because we're weak. In ever-increasing degrees He will work in us conformity to Christ the Redeemer. Let us take faith: God will help us.

THE VOICE OF LOVE

Let me take our statements of faith further and make our quest for discernment as practical as possible. *If we seek to know Christ's motives, we will soon perceive His thoughts, for thoughts exist to fulfill motives.* Christ's motive for coming to mankind is to reveal the Father's love. If we obtain His motive, we will increasingly hear His thoughts.

Thus, as we seek true discernment, let us make our steps practical by turning our focus upon Christ's love. Indeed, God's Word tells us that "faith work[s] through love" (Gal. 5:6). Our discernment is made more sure as we rest our heads upon Christ's breast and listen to His heart.

Yet I also acknowledge that, for some, to love as Christ has loved us remains an ideal too far to reach. Therefore let's start small and bring this task close to home. Rather than attempting to love everyone, let us reduce our challenge and determine to love just one person. Now I do not mean stop loving family or those you already love. I mean add just one person and love that individual in a greater way.

This person may be a lost neighbor or a backslidden friend; he or she might be a sick acquaintance or an elderly person from church or a child in pain. The Lord will lead you and help you reduce your goal to genuinely loving just one soul.

Come to this experiment without seeking to correct him or her, unless they themselves ask for advice. Pray daily for the individual. And as you listen to the voice of God's love, something inside you will flower and open naturally toward higher realms of discernment. Inspired by God, impulses and ideas born of love will increase in your relationship with others as well, and the knowledge and insights you gain from loving just one will become a natural part of your personality in loving many.

Yes, discernment will grow as you love just one.

7

FAST FROM JUDGING

If you have ever gone on an extended fast, you know it can be a life-changing experience. There are many types of fasts. The king of Nineveh along with the nobles and all the people of his nation fasted completely from food and water. The Lord heard the sincerity in their repentance and spared their nation, making them an example of how prayer, coupled with fasting, touched the heart of God (Jonah 3; Luke 11:32).

A fast can be a powerful tool to help stimulate revival or, conversely, it can degrade into a religious exercise that has almost no spiritual significance. The Pharisees fasted twice a week but did so to be seen of men. Their fast became a thing of religious pride. It was completely without spiritual value.

Examples of True Fasts

At its essence, the purpose of a fast is to help us reach our spiritual destination faster, hence the name *fast*. Jesus said "Blessed are those who hunger and thirst for righteousness, for they shall be satisfied" (Matt. 5:6). The goal of our hunger is for righteousness to prevail, either in us personally or in our family, church, city or nation. Fasting takes us there faster.

Yet we must not allow our fast to become a form of self-inflicted punishment. Fasting is not about "severe treatment of the body" (Col. 2:20–23). In truth, a fast is a gift of grace – an opportunity to engage the Lord in an extended time of desire. During the time you would have nourished your body, nourish yourself spiritually instead. Draw closer to the Lord. Read the Word of God, memorize Scriptures, or pray for yourself and others.

Isaiah 58 tells us that a fast can also be a time to show God's love to others. The Lord says,

> *"Is this not the fast which I choose, to loosen the bonds of wickedness, to undo the bands of the yoke, and to let the oppressed go free and break every yoke? Is it not to divide your bread with the hungry and bring the homeless poor into the house; when you see the naked, to cover him?"* —Isaiah 58:6–7

Therefore, when you are fasting from food, consider also ways to help the disadvantaged and hurting. You might even devote your food money to a relief agency who gives care to suffering people in destitute places.

THE INTERCESSOR'S FAST

From our study, we see that a fast can be a genuine form of seeking God, or it can be a shallow display of self-righteousness. The fast itself can be a denial of food or a specific food group, such as meats or desserts. Or it can be a denial of self, where we give ourselves to helping others less fortunate than ourselves (Isa. 58).

One aspect of the Isaiah 58 fast is seen in verse 9, which reads, "Remove the yoke from your midst, the pointing of the finger and speaking wickedness." This aspect of life, "the pointing of the finger and speaking wickedness," has become a normal part of our culture. Self-righteous judging, fault-finding, loveless criticisms and slander are all things that many Christians do without conscience or regret. If, however, we remove these things from our lives and give ourselves to a walk of love, the result is profound:

"Then your light will rise in darkness and your gloom will become like midday. And the Lord will continually guide you, and satisfy your

*desire in scorched places, and give strength to
your bones; and you will be like a watered garden, and like a spring of water whose waters
do not fail. Those from among you will rebuild
the ancient ruins; you will raise up the age-old
foundations; And you will be called the repair-
er of the breach, the restorer of the streets in
which to dwell."*   *—Isaiah 58:10–12*

I want to introduce a new concept: the fast from
judging. When I have mentioned this type of fast to
others, it is interesting to watch their reactions. "What
will we think about?" they query. I am not saying we
should fast from thinking. No, I am saying only this:
After we have thought about some issue of life, fast
from letting our concluding thoughts be those of judgment. Rather, let our thoughts end in prayer for mercy,
redemption and forgiveness.

You see, the instinct to judge and criticize is a curse
upon the church, and it brings death upon us as individuals. A curse? Death? Yes, every time we judge we
are simultaneously judged by God, and each time we
condemn another we ourselves are condemned (Matt.
7:1–2; Luke 6:37).

Many Christians will pray, engage in spiritual warfare, and rebuke the devil, yet often the enemy they
are fighting is not the devil. It is the harvest of what

they have sown with their own words and attitudes! It is consequential: *life measured back to us according to our attitudes toward others.*

When we judge and criticize, we position ourselves under judgment. You see, we are constantly sowing and harvesting life according to our own attitudes.

When I say "fast from judging," I do not mean we should abandon discernment. No. But judging people is not discernment. When we see something wrong, instead of only turning critical, we must learn to pray for mercy for that situation. We may still see what is wrong, but now we are harnessing our energies and seeking to redeem what is wrong by the power of Christ's love.

Jesus said, "Blessed are the merciful, for they shall receive mercy" (Matt. 5:7). When we resist the impulse to judge or condemn and instead pray for mercy, an amazing thing happens: *fresh mercy opens before us.* You see, in every moment of every day there are two paths in front of us: one leads to increased mercy in our lives while the other leads to a life of obstacles and difficulties. How do we receive more mercy? The key to a life blessed by God's mercy is to give mercy to those around us (Matt. 18:21–35).

There are Christians I know who have not made spiritual progress for years. They attend church and they tithe, yet they maintain a self-righteous, judgmental attitude. They always have something negative to say about others. As such, they position themselves under God's judgment. Their capacity to receive divine mercy is closed because they do not show mercy toward others.

James wrote: "Judgment will be merciless to one who has shown no mercy; mercy triumphs over judgment" (James 2:13). Let me repeat this sobering verse again: *"Judgment will be merciless to one who has shown no mercy."*

Are you pondering why your version of Christianity doesn't quite feel like the abundant life Jesus promised in John 10:10? Perhaps it is because you are too judgmental. It is a natural tendency in most people. Indeed, recall how even the Lord's disciples wanted to call fire down upon the Samaritans. Yet Jesus rebuked His disciples, saying that they did not know what spirit they were of (Luke 9:51–56). Let us, therefore, discern "what spirit" we are of. Let us remember that mercy triumphs over judgment; if we strive to be merciful, God promises He will respond to us as we have responded to others. Finally, let's ponder the next season of change. Perhaps it is time to embrace the mercy fast and see what changes occur in our lives when, for just ten days, we fast from judging.

8

Purity of Heart: Open Vision

Revelation Perception At the Throne of God

In the book of Revelation there is a marvel: "in the center and around the throne, four living creatures full of eyes in front and behind ... around and within" (Rev. 4:6, 8).

The Revelation of John is, by definition, a book of revelations. What John portrays in visions speaks a prophetic language that represents something deeper than that which is apparent. Thus, the myriad eyes of the living creatures that John saw at God's throne tell us a story, that "in the center and around [God's] throne" there exists multidimensional open vision. This is the meaning of the creatures "full of eyes in front and behind ... around and within."

If we desire true discernment, it will be measured to us naturally by our proximity to God's throne. *Nearness to God gives us clearness of vision.* And since only the pure in heart perceive God (Matt. 5:8), our goal is to possess the "sanctification without which no one will see the Lord" (Heb. 12:14).

Being spiritually reborn not only means the Spirit has entered our life on earth; we also have entered His life in Heaven. Thus, when Jesus spoke of being born again, He added a profound insight: being born of the Spirit is being born "from above" (John 3:3 AMP). Through the Holy Spirit, our spirits are positioned, raised up and seated with Christ in the heavenly places (Eph. 2:6). Where His presence is, there also is the authority of His throne, and in that place there is open vision.

In Him our eyes can think: they see with discernment and understanding. The mind of Christ fuses with our vision, revealing those things that were previously imperceptible. Not only do we perceive distant spiritual realities, but through the Holy Spirit we gain access to search "the depths of God" (1 Cor. 2:10). At the center of the throne is the majesty of the Almighty – adored by angels, worshipped by the redeemed. He sees the end from the beginning and knows all things. At the center of the throne, we know Him "who is and who was and who is to come" (Rev. 1:8), whose purposes cannot be thwarted.

Yet at the same time, being near to God also gives us "eyes ... within" (Rev. 4:8), inner eyes that monitor our motives and stand guard against sin. The more our vision opens up, the greater we see God in His holiness. The slightest sin in our lives becomes significant; we are compelled to live pure before Him.

The "four living creatures" at the throne of God do not cease to say, "Holy, Holy, Holy is the Lord God, the Almighty" (Rev. 4:8). Day and night, God is holy. When our spiritual eyes are open, the utterances of our mouths are all "holy, holy, holy."

A TRUE ISRAELITE HAS SPIRITUAL PERCEPTION

Jesus spoke concerning Nathanael, "Behold, an Israelite indeed, in whom there is no deceit!" (John 1:47). What kind of man was this disciple, that Jesus should praise him? There was no guile, no deceit in this young man's heart. Oh, how we should desire this purity for ourselves! Nathanael had "eyes ... within." He kept himself free from self-deception. When you cleave to the truth inwardly, you will perceive the truth outwardly. Nathanael looked at Jesus and declared, "You are the Son of God; You are the King of Israel" (v. 49).

Jesus said to Nathanael, "You will see greater things than these.... I say to you, you will see the heavens opened and the angels of God ascending and descending on the Son of Man" (vv. 50–51). Because of Nathanael's honesty of heart, Jesus knew open vision would be inevitable. *Open vision is the consequence of a pure heart.* To those who fight against sin, who hate falsehood, who diligently pursue walking in holiness, your struggle is a preparation for seeing God. You shall see the heavens opened.

Yet because of dullness of heart, most have come to expect spiritual blindness as an unfortunate condition of this world. The truth is, in the Old Testament one of God's judgments against sinners was that the heavens became "bronze" (Deut. 28:23). Most Christians similarly see the heavens closed. Few see with open vision either into the heavenly realms or into their own hearts.

The heavens are always "bronze" to a hardened heart.

However, as the Lord promised Nathanael that he would "see the heavens opened," so Christ desires us to have true spiritual vision. One sign that the Holy Spirit is involved in a church is that "your young men ... see visions, and your old men ... dream dreams" (Acts 2:17). There is continuity between God's kingdom in Heaven and His kingdom on earth.

Oh, there are those who say the supernatural was strictly limited to the first century, that today we "walk by faith, not by sight" (2 Cor. 5:7). Yes, we often do take steps of faith, where we walk without prior knowledge of what each step involves. But do we not also perceive Him who is with us? Ours is not a blind trust; it is a proven, seeing trust! Walking by faith and having spiritual vision are not terms in conflict. Consider: moments before Paul stated he walked by faith, he wrote, "We look ... at the things which are not seen ... things which are ... eternal" (2 Cor. 4:18).

Paul had revelation perception of the spirit realm. He saw the eternal spiritual body that was prepared and waiting for him in the heavens! (2 Cor. 5:1–4). He knew how "a man ... was caught up into Paradise and heard inexpressible words" (2 Cor. 12:3–4). It is amazing to me, but Paul had no mentor besides Jesus. He could not read Romans or Ephesians to build a sermon. The truth of God was unveiled to him in unbroken streams of revelation. Paul authored one-third of the New Testament out of his open vision of Christ. How did he see the things he saw?

Perhaps the answer is in seeking purity of heart. Indeed, just after he declared, "With unveiled face, [we behold] ... the glory of the Lord" (2 Cor. 3:18), he wrote, "But we have renounced the things hidden because of shame" (2 Cor. 4:2). Later he continued,

"Having these promises, beloved, let us cleanse ourselves from all defilement of flesh and spirit, perfecting holiness in the fear of God" (2 Cor. 7:1). Out of a purified heart, out of perfected holiness, came open vision of the glory of God.

Remember, we are not seeking experiences; we are seeking a pure heart. We are not running after visions; we want holiness. Even as the supernatural realm was an expected phenomenon in the primitive church, so also was purity the expected condition in their hearts.

Therefore do not be as the foolish ones who seek to conjure up visions. You must seek sanctification, and when you are ready, the Lord will speak to you in supernatural ways (Acts 2:17–18). Seek to have a clean heart, allowing Christ to examine and purge you daily. As He washes you with His Word and chastens you with His holiness, He will draw you into His presence. He will open your eyes to things around and things within.

—Adapted from *Holiness, Truth*
and the Presence of God

9

RIGHTEOUS JUDGMENT

In the preceding chapters I have urged you, my friends and colleagues, to resist the trends of self-righteous anger, judgmentalism, and bitter cynicism that exist in our world today. Instead, let us seek to possess the "higher ... thoughts" of Christ (Isa. 55:9).

In truth, our calling is to serve God as ambassadors of Christ (Eph. 6:20). A true ambassador is not only pledged to represent his or her leader; the ambassador is one who knows what that ruler actually thinks and what he would say. He receives regular communication with that leader and is current on his leader's short-term and long-term goals. Should the ambassador be ignorant of the ruler's view, he is trained to not offer his own opinions; he is to wait until he hears from the one he represents. The world doesn't want to know what we think. There are some seven billion opinions in the world today; what the nations need is not to hear our opinions but to hear the One we represent: our King, Jesus Christ.

I have also endeavored to put a roadblock in front of false discernment. We must avoid the self-righteous, religious approach of the Pharisees. When I urge people to not be judgmental, I am not saying, don't discern. Spiritual discernment is an art form, while judging by outer appearance is an instinct of the flesh. I am saying we must learn how to wait, listen and, in meekness, discern the higher way of Christ.

Judgment That Is Righteous

Yet inevitably there are still questions. What about the Lord's admonition calling us to "not judge according to appearance, but judge with righteous judgment" (John 7:24)? What is righteous judgment?

In discussing this with others, I've noticed that the words *righteous* and *judgment* seem to be all that some read in the verse. However, the first part of the verse explains, at least partially, the second half: righteous judgment is that which is "not ... according to appearance." Righteous judgment comes from another source, that which is higher than the instincts of the flesh.

You see, there is a difference between discerning a need that you are determined to pray for and, in contrast, simply finding fault, which often degrades into gossip and slander. God does not call a person into a "ministry of judging others" just because such a one has always been fearless to "tell it as it is." Faultfinding is not a gift of the Spirit.

If your judgment is truly from God, it will not be an isolated gift. You will also have humility from God, love, and lowliness of mind.

Righteous judgment proves itself genuine by the virtues that support and present it.

All the virtues of the Spirit – love, joy, peace, gentleness, etc. – should be functionally evident in your character. If so, you will be known to be gentle, loving, lowly of mind and wise. When you bring a righteous judgment, your character affirms that your judgment is not an emotional reaction, but you come as one sent from God – like Christ, you are typically full of grace and truth. You speak as an individual who is seriously concerned with bettering the lives of others.

As John wrote,

By this, love is perfected with us, so that we may have confidence in the day of judgment; because as He is, so also are we in this world.
—1 John 4:17

Yes, the day of judgment is coming. Our goal should be that "love is perfected with us." In the seasons of judgment, we are called to a life of perfect love, for "as He is, so also are we in this world."

10

REMEMBER JOB

Before I conclude this first section, I would like to relate a story about a Bible hero of mine. His name is Job. According to the Lord, Job was the most righteous man on earth. He was not just a relatively good man among other good men, but among all men there was "no one like him on the earth." In God's eyes Job was in a class by himself: three times he was called a "blameless and upright man" by God (Job 1:1, 8; 2:3).

The Lord not only knew Job, but all the people in his city knew him as well. His reputation was impeccable and well known. God had personally worked character in Job's nature and blessed His servant with all the rewards of the righteous.

However, Satan also knew Job and had tried numerous times to entice him to sin, but failed. In Satan's travels upon the earth, he knew men well: men might appear righteous, but only if their righteousness came with a reward.

"Does Job fear God for nothing?" Satan taunted. "Have You not made a hedge about him and his house and all that he has, on every side? You have blessed the work of his hands, and his possessions have increased in the land. But put forth Your hand now and touch all that he has; he will surely curse You to Your face" (Job 1:9–12).

So this challenge became the basis of a test: With everything Job loved taken from him, would he still serve God if he received nothing in return? Would he continue to revere the Almighty even in the face of great loss?

In spite of the catastrophic calamities that Satan levied against Job – and in spite of the confusion and dismay Job experienced – Job did not curse God. He passed the test; he endured a most severe satanic attack and did not turn away from God. He did not understand what was occurring or why, but without the hedge of divine blessings, even under extreme sufferings, Job's character protected him from turning away from the Lord. Not only was God glorified, but Satan was humiliated.

Since the time of Job's life, perhaps billions of people have found comfort and courage by studying the life of Job. He is not only a great hero upon earth but also in Heaven. I'm sure that God Himself has rewarded Job in ways unimaginable, and that in Heaven Job's suffering has produced for him an eternal weight of glory far beyond all comparison. I'm also convinced that both sets of Job's children, plus Job's wife, experienced unspeakable joy when they met each other on the eternal shore.

THE STORY WITHIN THE STORY

There is much to say about the book of Job. Many scholars believe it is the oldest book of the Bible; all agree that it predates the wisdom books (Proverbs, Psalms, etc.) Another interesting insight is this: Job was not an Israelite. So the antiquity of this book combined with its Gentile background makes it unique among all Old Testament Scriptures.

Yet there is another narrative that is actually my main point of interest. The story of Job is not only about an innocent man suffering unjustly from a satanic attack; the bulk of the story concerns the suffering Job endured from his three friends, Eliphaz, Bildad and Zophar (and later Elihu). These men, religious scholars of their day, were friends of Job who during his distress became his accusers.

In defense of Job's friends, upon seeing Job's great suffering they threw dust on their heads and wept. Then they sat with him in silence for the next seven days. Only after Job spoke did they finally open their mouths in response. They began with reverence, weeping, and compassion (a place we might consider taking before we offer our opinions!). However, it is plain that their religious opinions outweighed their sympathies toward Job.

Additionally, it must be noted that the basis of their accusations rested upon generally true biblical principles. Variations of their perspectives, in fact, were later quoted by such luminaries as David, Solomon, Isaiah and others in the Old Testament, and Paul in the New Testament (compare Job 5:13; 1 Cor. 3:19, etc.). Nothing in their general views was contrary to truths published elsewhere in the Bible. The problem was not with their doctrines but with their application. If Job was a sinner, most of what they had said would be applicable, but he wasn't a sinner. He was the most righteous man on earth. Job's friends had right doctrines that were wrongly applied, and in their religious pride they did not have enough humility to see they could be wrong.

We all have read the book of Job. We know that what happened to Job came from the devil and that the Lord's view of Job was that Job was blameless. We all also know it was wrong of Job's friends to falsely judge him. Yet still, people today cannot help but find fault with this godly man!

If we read some modern interpretations of the book of Job, we find critics are still blaming Job for his suffering – some say Job's devastation occurred because of unbelief; others say his fear opened the door to the adversary (Job 3). And still others feel Job must have had some sin that left him vulnerable to the devil's attack. How is it that people cannot see this stunning reality: NONE of the things spoken against Job – not 3,500 years ago nor today – were right!

The instinct to judge and criticize without having all the information is rampant in the world. Unfortunately, it is also in us, Christ's church. If we think Job caused his own troubles, then we are as deceived as the three who counseled him. In fact, we are worse, because they did not know Satan was behind the attack or that God had declared Job blameless. On the other hand, we have the written testimony of God. Yet in spite of what we can plainly read, our religious minds hunger to find fault.

Could it be that the take-away message of the book of Job – the reason it is in the Bible in the first place – is to provide a vivid example that it is wrong to judge without knowing all the facts? Indeed, the book of Job is a portrait of people with a religious mindset who are self-assured they are right, who judge without having heard from God.

Perhaps the main message to us from this book should be: do not judge Job!

God placed the life story of Job in the most sacred Book in the world for a reason: that we would not be so confident that our judgments are always right. The fact is, throughout history good people, godly people, have been lied about, slandered, blamed and persecuted! We know the wicked suffer, but do we take into account that so also do the righteous? And that the main accusers of the righteous are not necessarily the openly godless in the world, but more often the self-righteous religious leaders of the day?

Job's friends had right doctrines that were wrongly applied. In their religious pride they did not have enough humility to see they could be wrong.

In Conclusion

As we bring Part One to a close, I want to say with peace and grace upon my words that we must crucify our instincts to judge. When Job's relatives came, they invested in Job with love and gifts. They restored him. They did not come with a religious instinct to probe and pick at Job's soul for hidden sin. They did what love would do.

Of course, there are people who have sinned, who have done things morally and legally wrong. Beloved, I am not saying we should not deal with these problems. Of course, if you see criminal action – theft or injustice of some kind that is unmistakably evil – yes, judge by "outer appearance" and inner conviction. Act to bring swift justice. But in most cases these things are not so obvious. Therefore, I make my appeal to you: before you judge, remember Job and why his story is in the Bible.

When I look back at the many times I was foolish or angry or just sinful in some way, I recall that Jesus Christ has never stood to condemn me; He has always reached down to lift me. I have always been lifted and cleansed by His love and grace.

As He has been to us, so we can be to others. We can possess the very same "mind … which was also in Christ Jesus" (Phil. 2:5 KJV).

PART TWO

DISCERNING
OF SPIRITS

Remember, dear man or woman of God,
you are called to follow Christ
the Redeemer!
Therefore, you must not confuse
the voice of the prison guard
with the voice of the imprisoned.
Never forget, the heart of Christ
is to set captives free.

For our struggle is not
against flesh and blood,
but against the rulers, against the powers,
against the world forces of this darkness,
against the spiritual forces of wickedness
in the heavenly places.

— EPHESIANS 6:12 —

11

Holy Spirit Radar

For nothing is hidden that will not become evident, nor anything secret that will not be known and come to light. —*Luke 8:17*

The peace of Christ is not just a divine attribute; it is also an organ of communication in the language of God. The Holy Spirit uses peace to communicate with us. If a situation warrants caution, our peace is troubled; if a direction is rightly chosen, peace confirms it. Thus, we are admonished by God's Word to "let the peace of Christ rule in [our] hearts" (Col. 3:15). The literal translation for *rule* is "to act as arbiter."

As we debate in our souls a course of action, Christ's peace acts like a spiritual radar. It helps make our powers of discernment more effective.

When we first were born again, it was not to a religion that we gave our hearts; it was to Christ through the Holy Spirit. The Spirit of God actually entered our lives, and with Him came His inner witness of peace. This is not a little thing, for the Gospel is actually called the "Gospel of Peace" (Eph. 6:15).

Of course, the "circuitry" that makes our spirit-guidance system accurate is our knowledge of God's Word. We must, therefore, be grounded in God's Word. We are not discussing a psychic ability but a spiritual faculty that is part of our relationship with Christ.

Scripture says that Jesus was "aware in His spirit" of the thoughts and motives of others (Mark 2:8). So again, the faculty we want to develop is a spiritual thing, not soulish – and definitely not something borrowed from the occult.

Coupled with the Word of God, your radar can be a type of scanner that actually discerns hidden issues or danger. Thus, you can trust the Holy Spirit's guidance to help you recognize what may be troubling you in your spirit.

For example, I was conducting a Bible study on a college campus when a young man came into the room, sat down and joined us. Outwardly he appeared clean-cut but I felt cautioned by my inner radar, so I stopped the Bible study and asked him openly if he were involved in witchcraft or the occult. He said no. However, even though he was clean-cut, the warning in my spirit wouldn't go away. I asked again, and again he denied any connections to witchcraft. I felt the Holy Spirit focus upon his coat pocket, so I asked him what was in his coat pocket. This time he answered honestly, pulling two chicken claws out of his pocket. He had just been to an occult ritual. His response now was more humble, and we were able to actually pray with him for salvation before we left.

Some say that God doesn't speak to them, but this is not true. They just haven't learned the language of the Spirit. When the Holy Spirit comes, He brings communication with Heaven: dreams, visions and prophecies all represent union with God. Therefore, you must believe God can get through to you. What you need is the ability to interpret the influences of God upon your spirit. To sense what the Spirit of God is saying to you is, at its essence, the source of true spiritual discernment. In this regard, it is good to remember John's words:

> *These things I have written to you concerning those who are trying to deceive you. As for you, the anointing which you received from Him abides in you, and you have no need for anyone to teach you; but as His anointing teaches you about all things, and is true and is not a*

*lie, and just as it has taught you, you abide in
Him.*   *—1 John 2:26–27*

So let's put this into perspective: we have an inner witness that gives us peace while helping us decide and discern. This "peace connection" does not, however, allow us to ignore input from leaders or others whom God may use. While we must maintain sovereignty over our will, God gives us ministries to train and equip us (Eph. 4:11–12). That said, it is the anointing of the Holy Spirit that is the final amen to the truth of God.

Our goal is to develop that inner witness, for when it is united with knowledge of the Word of God, we have a powerful resource added to our arsenal of faith. Remember, the Spirit and the Word always agree. So if you memorize and study the Word of God and walk in the Spirit, you will increasingly possess discernment.

12

DISCERNING
THE SPIRIT OF JEZEBEL

We are going to confront a stronghold of immense proportions. It is a way of thinking that exists unchecked in most churches. Therefore, let us expose and then destroy the hiding places of Jezebel.

UNDERSTANDING THE SPIRIT OF JEZEBEL

But I have this against you, that you tolerate the woman Jezebel, who calls herself a prophetess, and she teaches and leads My bond-servants astray so that they commit acts of immorality and eat things sacrificed to idols.

—Revelation 2:20

You may challenge addressing the above quote to American churches. You may argue that no one in your church openly instructs people to commit acts of immorality. I understand your sense of alarm. I agree that you probably know of no one who brazenly preaches that sexual lust and idolatry are not sins. When we speak of Jezebel, we are identifying the source in our society of obsessive sensuality, unbridled witchcraft, and hatred for male authority.

To understand the spirit of Jezebel, we must understand the genesis of this personality in the Bible. The first mention of Jezebel is seen in the rebellious, manipulative wife of King Ahab. It was actually this spirit, operating through Queen Jezebel, that had caused millions of Israelites from the northern ten tribes – all but seven thousand faithful souls – to bow to Baal. Under her control, these people had forsaken the covenant, destroyed the sacred altars, and killed the prophets (1 Kings 19). Think of it! This one spirit was almost totally responsible for corrupting an entire nation. And it is this principality that today has come full force against our nation.

Jezebel is fiercely independent and intensely ambitious for pre-eminence and control. Jezebel will not dwell with anyone unless she can control and dominate the relationship. When she seems submissive or servant-like, it is only for the sake of gaining some strategic advantage. From her heart, she yields to no one.

Bear in mind that the spirit that produced Jezebel existed before its namesake was born. Although we refer to Jezebel as "she," this spirit is without gender. However, it is important to note that Jezebel is more attracted to the uniqueness of the female psyche in its sophisticated ability to manipulate without physical force.

Look for Jezebel to target women who are embittered against men either through neglect or misuse of authority. This spirit operates through women who, because of insecurity, jealousy or vanity, desire to control and dominate others. Jezebel is behind the woman who publicly humiliates her husband with her tongue and then thereafter controls him by his fear of public embarrassment.

While she uses every means of sexual perversity known in hell, immorality is not the issue; *control* is what she seeks, using the power of sexual passions for the purpose of possessing men. To a woman under the influence of Jezebel, *conquering* a man need not involve physical contact if a seductive glance of her eyes will capture him.

THE BATTLE HAS EXPANDED

Since the era of the early apostles, and especially since the dawn of the electronic age, the scale of battle has greatly enlarged. It is difficult for us in our generation to discern the scope of warfare that hits the church and the world in general. We might actually suppose that warfare should decrease as the number of demons has not changed since the first century, while mankind has grown from 150 million in the apostolic age to more than seven billion souls today. Yet the access the devil has to the souls in our world has increased through the mass communications media and literature. John wrote of this period in time in Revelation 12:15: "And the serpent poured water like a river out of his mouth after the woman, so that he might cause her [the church] to be swept away with the flood."

Water, in this context, symbolizes "words." In our world there exists a flood of *words* and *visual images* coming out of the mouth of Satan. Our society, through technological advances, has made sins of the mind and heart more accessible. More than ever before, the carnal mind, with its openness to this satanic flood of filth and rebellion, is being structured into a powerful stronghold for the devil.

In our information-filled, entertainment-oriented world, even minor demons can exercise major influence simply by possessing the scriptwriters and producers of movies and television. Indeed, Satan has always been "the prince of the power of the air" (Eph. 2:2). But we should realize that the "power of the air" is not merely the wind; in our world this power uniquely includes the electronic airwaves that carry communication and entertainment signals.

Therefore, we must discern exactly where the satanic inroads are in our own lives and cut them off. We cannot worship God Sunday morning and then tolerate Jezebel through immoral entertainment Sunday night. Indeed, it is in regard to warring against Jezebel that Jesus described Himself as, "He who searches the minds and hearts" (Rev. 2:23). For it is in the inner sanctuary of our soul life where tolerance to Jezebel begins. It is here, within us, where tolerance must end.

SET THE CAPTIVES FREE!

Jezebel's spirit flows unhindered throughout the entertainment industries. It flaunts itself in the world of fashion; it holds degrees in the philosophical departments of our schools and colleges. Where can you go in our society that the influence of this spirit is not felt? She is the destroyer of politician and preacher alike. She is the cruel motivator behind abortion. It is Jezebel who frequently generates dissatisfaction between spouses.

This spirit was sitting in the church in Thyatira when the Holy Spirit exposed it two thousand years ago (Rev. 2:20). It still has its favorite seat in church today. There are respectable men who love God and who seek to serve Him, yet secretly in their hearts they are prisoners of Jezebel. Even now they are deeply ashamed of their bondage to pornography, and they can barely control their desires for women. Ask them to pray and their spirits are awash with guilt and shame. Their prayers are but the whimpers of Jezebel's eunuchs.

There are good women who come to church seeking God, but this spirit has them fantasizing about the men in their assembly – lamenting that their husbands are not as *spiritual* as other husbands. Soon these women develop problems that *only the male pastor* can understand. Ladies, the "older women" (Titus 2:3–5) – the *godly* women in the church – are the ones you need to consult with first, not the pastor or elders. If you must counsel with a male pastor, do not be offended when he asks for his wife or an older, godly woman to join him.

Anyone who is hit by this spirit needs first to repent deeply of their sympathetic thoughts toward it, and then war against it! Do not waste days and weeks under condemnation. Separate yourself from that Jezebelian thinking that was fostered upon you in your youth. Pick up the sword of the Spirit and war against the spirit of Jezebel! Pray for the saints in your church. Pray for the Christians throughout your community. *If you war against Jezebel when you are tempted, eventually you are going to become dangerous.* This spirit will stop attacking you once it recognizes that your aggressive counterattack is setting other people free.

Likely Targets

We have stated that this spirit prefers to exploit the more complex nature of a woman, yet this demon can also operate through men. In fact, Jezebel seeks the highly refined qualities of the professional musician, especially when such a man has both the ambition and the opportunity to become a worship leader or director. It will also seek to surface in the life of the pastor himself, in which case he will become very authoritarian and unyielding in his control of the church. Such a pastor will invariably be isolated from fellowship and accountability with other pastors. He will find himself lured into maintaining flirtatious and sensual relationships – "special intimacies" – with one or more women in the church. In time, he will most likely succumb to adultery.

Yet this spirit more often seeks the sophistication of the feminine nature, especially when that woman's ambition is to be widely recognized in ministry. Remember, Jesus said of Jezebel, "[She] calls herself a prophetess" (Rev. 2:20). A woman can most certainly function prophetically (Acts 2:17); she can be

85

anointed and commission by God to serve with authority as a prophetess (Acts 21:8–9). But when she insists
upon recognition, when she manipulates or entirely
disregards the established leadership in the church and
builds her own following – when she "calls herself a
prophetess" – we should be concerned.

Let me also say that the antidote for this spirit is
not a distant commodity; the remedy is humility, along
with trusting God and making ourselves accountable
to others. Remember, this spirit especially targets
prayer leaders, church secretaries, worship and song
leaders, and pastors and their spouses – each according to their own vulnerability. People serving in these
roles should be reminded that humility is the armor
that keeps the enemy at bay. Leaders should be trained
to discern and war against the spirit of Jezebel.

WHAT JEZEBEL HATES

Jezebel hates repentance. Her worst fear is that the
people will begin to mourn over their sins. Though
this spirit will infiltrate the church, masking its desire
for control with true Christian doctrines, it will hide
from true repentance.

Jezebel hates humility. Jesus taught that greatness
in the kingdom was measured in childlike honesty of
heart, not in what we appear to be to others. *A true*

ministry is willing and eager to be submitted and accountable to other ministries. It is typical of those who are servant-minded. Therefore, we must learn that spirituality is measured in meekness, not intellectual power.

Jezebel hates prayer. Intercessory prayer pries her fingers off the hearts and souls of men. It sets people free in the spirit. When you pray, it binds her. When you pray against immorality, it cripples her. When you pray for a submissive heart, it is like the trampling of Jehu's horse upon her body.

Jezebel hates the prophets, for the prophets speak out against her. The prophets are her worst enemies. When she wars, it is to stir people against the message of the prophetic church. Yet more than her hatred for the prophetic ministry, she hates the words they speak. Her real enemy is the spoken Word of God.

Jezebel's ultimate hatred is against God Himself. She hates the grace God lavishes upon His bond-servants, even after they sin. She hates the fact that God will take the weakest and lowliest and use them to bring her down. She hates the holiness and purity of heart that comes from God and surrounds those who serve in His courts.

Let's pray: *Father, we submit to You and Your standard of righteousness. We ask for purity, meekness,*

87

and holiness of heart. Forgive us for our tolerance of the spirit of Jezebel in both our minds and our deeds.

Father, because we submit to You, we have Your authority to resist the devil. We bind, in the name of Jesus, the spirit of Jezebel. We pray against the stronghold of Jezebelian thinking over our community and our state. We come against the fortresses this demon has built up in the spirit realm in this area, and we ask the Holy Spirit to plunder the house of Jezebel and distribute her goods.

We also pray for faithfulness of eyes and hearts for husbands and wives. We release purity of heart and grace to each member of the body of Christ, both single and married. We cover Your people with the blood of Jesus. We loose the joy of a humble and submissive spirit and pull down the imaginations of ambition and pride. In Jesus' name. Amen!

—Adapted from *The Three Battlegrounds*

13

EXPOSING THE ACCUSER OF THE BRETHREN

More churches have been destroyed by the accuser of the brethren and its faultfinding than by either immorality or misuse of church funds. So prevalent is this influence in our society that, among many, faultfinding has been elevated to the status of a "ministry"! The Lord has promised, however, that in His house accusing one another will be replaced with prayer, and faultfinding will be replaced with a love that covers a multitude of sins.

SATAN WANTS TO STOP YOUR GROWTH

Let me preface this chapter by saying that there are times when a pastor or church ministry falls into serious sin. In those cases, if they have repented, a restoration team would need to handle that situation wisely, discerning the most appropriate approach for healing the church and redeeming the failure. If a leader sins, he or she will need to step out of ministry and follow the restoration process assigned to them. We must act with righteousness in mind. Those who have blatantly sinned before all should be rebuked before all if they refuse to accept correction.

However, bear in mind that no one is perfect. There will always be issues between Christians that will need godly remedies but not necessarily dismissal. Until Jesus comes, we will have to cover one another and approach correction, when it is necessary, with a gentle spirit.

There is, however, another time when minimal issues or flaws are exaggerated by the enemy to sow strife and division in the church. In an attempt to hinder if not altogether halt the next move of God, Satan has sent forth an army of faultfinding demons against the church. The purpose of this assault is to entice the body of Christ away from the perfection of Jesus and onto the imperfections of one another.

The faultfinder spirit's assignment is to assault relationships on all levels. It attacks families, churches and interchurch associations, seeking to bring irreparable schisms into our unity. Masquerading as discernment, this spirit will slip into our opinions of other people; it will leave us critical and judgmental. Consequently, we all need to evaluate our attitude toward others. If our thoughts are other than "faith working through love" (Gal. 5:6), we need to be aware that we may be under spiritual attack.

The faultfinder demon will incite individuals to spend days and even weeks unearthing old faults or sins in their minister or church. The people who are held captive by this deceitful spirit become "crusaders," irreconcilable enemies of their former assemblies. In many cases, the things they deem wrong or lacking are the very areas in which the Lord seeks to position them for intercession. What might otherwise be an opportunity for spiritual growth and meeting a need becomes an occasion of stumbling and withdrawal. In truth, their criticisms are a smoke screen for a prayerless heart and an unwillingness to serve.

That someone should discover the imperfections of their pastor or church is by no means a sign of spirituality. Indeed, we could find fault with the church even before we were Christians. There is a difference between a self-righteous, critical spirit and the grace and truth of the Holy Spirit. What we do with what we see, however, is the measure of Christlike maturity. Remember, when Jesus saw the condition of mankind, He identified with humanity, took the form of man, and then died for our sins (Phil. 2:7–8). He didn't condemn us; He died for us. Paul's admonition is that we "have this attitude in [ourselves] which was also in Christ Jesus" (v. 5).

No One Is Exempt

It is of some consolation that Christ Himself could not measure up to the "standards" of this faultfinding spirit when it attacked Him through the Pharisees. No matter what Jesus did, the Pharisees found fault with Him. If you personally have not consulted with and listened to the individual of whom you are critical, how can you be sure that you are not fulfilling the role of the accuser of the brethren? Even the "Law does not judge a man unless it first hears from him" (John 7:51).

The enemy's purpose in this assault is to discredit the minister so it can discredit his message. I have personally listened to scores of pastors from many denominational backgrounds, and I have found that the timing of this spirit's attack upon their congregations was most frequently just prior to or immediately after a significant breakthrough. The unchallenged assault of this demon always stopped the forward progress of their church.

When this spirit infiltrates an individual's mind, its accusations come with such venom and intimidation that even those who should know better are bewildered and then seduced by its influence. Nearly all involved take their eyes off Jesus and focus upon "issues," ignoring during the contention that Jesus is actually praying for His body to become one.

Beguiled by this demon, accusations and counter-accusations rifle through the soul of the congregation, stimulating suspicion and fear among the people. Weariness and devastation wracks the targeted ministry, while discouragement blankets the pastor, his family, and other servants of God in the church.

Nearly every believer reading this has faced the assault of the faultfinder spirit at one time or another. Each has known the depression of trying to track down this accusing spirit as it whispers its gossip through the local church: trusted friends seem distant, established relationships are shaken, and the vision of the church is in a quagmire of strife and inaction.

Admittedly, as I said earlier, there are individuals and ministries in which serious sin or heresy has been blatantly manifest. These things need confrontation and correction, but even here the process should begin with Christ's instructions in Matthew 18:15–17. Ultimately, those who refuse correction and continue to sin before all should be rebuked and even put out of the church if need be. But even here the rebuke should not be without prayer and compassion for all involved. Remember also, there are denominational supervisors as well as local ministerial associations that can review disputes privately.

To mask the diabolical nature of its activity, the faultfinder spirit will often garb its criticisms in religious clothing. Under the pretense of protecting sheep from a "gnat-sized" error in doctrine, it forces the flock to swallow a "camel-sized" error of loveless correction. In an attempt to correct violations of Scripture, the very methods employed are a violation of Scripture! Where is the "spirit of gentleness" of which Paul speaks in Galatians 6:1, the humility in "looking to yourself, so that you too will not be tempted"? Where is the love motive to "restore such a one"?

In most cases the person supposedly in error has never even been contacted before his alleged mistakes enter the rumor mill of the city's churches or media outlets. Only then, after the slander has been made public through a book, CD or broadcast, does he become aware of his alleged faults. Brethren, the spirit behind such accusations must be discerned, for its motive is not to restore and heal but to destroy.

THE PURE EXAMPLE

The church does need correction, and ministers and public leaders need accountability, but the ministry of reproof must be patterned after Christ and not the accuser of the brethren. When Jesus corrected the churches in Asia (Rev. 2–3), He positioned His rebuke between praise and promises. He reassured the churches that the voice about to expose their sin was the very voice that inspired their virtue. After encouraging them, He then brought correction.

Even when a church was steeped in error, as was the case with two of the seven churches, Christ still offered grace for change. How patient was Jesus? He even gave "Jezebel ... time to repent" (Rev. 2:20–21). After He admonished a church, His last words were not condemnation but promises.

Is this not His way with each of us? Even in the most serious corrections, the voice of Jesus is always the embodiment of "grace and truth" (John 1:14). Jesus said of the sheep, "They know his voice. A stranger they simply will not follow, but will flee from him" (John 10:4–5). Remember, if the word of rebuke or correction does not offer grace for restoration, it is not the voice of your Shepherd. If you are one of Christ's sheep, you will flee from it.

—Adapted from *When the Many Are One*

14

THE ENEMY'S WEAPONS

To find an indictment against the church, it is important to note that the enemy must draw his accusations from hell. If we have repented of our sins, no record of them or our mistakes exists in Heaven. As it is written, "Who will bring a charge against God's elect? God is the one who justifies" (Rom. 8:33). The Lord's covenant promise is that "their sins and their lawless deeds I will remember no more" (Heb. 10:17). Even while the Lord will speak to us of our sin and need of repentance, He is not condemning us. Rather, He is at the Father's right hand interceding on our behalf.

Let us, therefore, expose the weapons of the fault-finder spirit. The first weapon used against us is our unrepentant sins. Our failure to repent when the Holy

Spirit desires to correct us opens the door for the accuser to condemn us. You will recognize the voice of the enemy for it never offers hope or extends grace for repentance. It acts as though it is the voice of God and we are guilty of the "unpardonable sin." The way to defeat the enemy in this arena is to disarm him by sincerely repenting of the sin, confessing it to someone trustworthy, and then looking again to the atonement of Christ as the source of all our righteousness.

Yet Satan seeks not only to accuse us as individuals but to blend into our minds criticisms and condemnation against others as well. Instead of praying for one another, we react in the flesh against offenses. Our un-Christlike responses are then easily manipulated by the faultfinder spirit.

Therefore, we cast down the accuser of the brethren by learning to *pray for* one another instead of *preying on* one another. We must learn to forgive in the same manner as Christ has forgiven us. If one has repented of his sins, we must exercise the same attitude of "divine forgetfulness" that exists in Heaven. We defeat the faultfinder when we emulate the nature of Jesus: as a lamb Christ died for sinners; as a priest He intercedes.

The second weapon this demon uses against us is our past mistakes and poor decisions. Each of us has an inherent propensity toward ignorance. One does not have to read far into the history of the saints to discover they were not called because of their intrinsic wisdom. In truth, we all have made mistakes. Hopefully we have at least learned from them and developed humility because of them. This faultfinding demon, however, takes our past mistakes and parades them before our memory, criticizing our efforts to do God's will, thus keeping us in bondage to the past.

When the enemy pits us against one another, it first provokes us to jealousy or fear. The security of our place in life seems threatened by another's success. Perhaps to justify our personal failures or flaws, we magnify the past shortcomings of others. The more our jealousy grows, the more this demon exploits our thoughts, until nothing about the individual or his church seems right.

In the final stage, we actually wage a campaign against him. No defense he offers will satisfy us. We are convinced he is deceived and dangerous, and we think it is up to us to warn others. Yet the truth is that the person whose mind is controlled by the faultfinder demon is the one who is deceived and dangerous. His own unrepentant thoughts toward jealousy and fleshly criticism have supplied hell with a "lumberyard" of material to erect walls between members of the body of Christ.

Sadly, it is often leaders who have fallen from the intensity of their first love for Christ who become the fiercest persecutors of others who are seeking to possess more of the Holy Spirit. Christ's disciples will be persecuted, but I can find no biblical authorization for Christians to persecute other Christians. Persecution is a deed of the flesh. "As at that time he who was born according to the flesh persecuted him who was born according to the Spirit, so it is now also" (Gal. 4:29). Incredibly, those who are given to persecuting others actually think they are "offering service to God" (John 16:2).

To combat this enemy, we must create an atmosphere of grace among us as individuals and between us as churches. Like the Father who has given us life, we must seek to cause all things to work together for good. If one stumbles, we must be quick to cover him, without going so far as to create a false "cover-up" where we actually condone sin or hypocrisy. Yet we proceed with the knowledge that we are "members of one another" (Eph. 4:25). As it is written, "None of you shall approach any blood relative of his to uncover nakedness; I am the Lord" (Lev. 18:6). We are family, begotten from one Father. "Their nakedness you shall not uncover; for their nakedness is yours" (v. 10). Even under the old covenant it was unlawful to uncover another's "nakedness" publicly. Love finds a redemptive way to cover a multitude of sins.

WHERE THE VULTURES ARE GATHERED

The accuser uses yet another weapon, and it uses this weapon astutely. There are times in our walk with God when, to increase fruitfulness, the Father prunes us back (John 15:1–11). This season of pruning is actually one of preparation; the Lord's purpose is to lead His servants into new power in ministry.

During a time of pruning, God requires new levels of surrender as well as a fresh crucifixion of the flesh. It is often a time of humiliation and testing, of emptiness and seeming ineffectiveness as God expands and deepens our dependency upon Him. It can be a fearful time when our need is exposed in stark visibility.

Unfortunately, not only is this time of weakness apparent to the man or woman of God, but it also frequently occurs before the church and before principalities and powers. The faultfinder spirit and those who have come to think as it thinks find in their target's vulnerability an opportunity to crush him.

Time and again, what would otherwise have become an incubator of life becomes a coffin of death. Those who might otherwise emerge with the clarity and power of prophetic vision are beaten down and abandoned, cut off from the very people who should have prayed them through to resurrection. In this attack the faultfinder is most destructive. For here this demon aborts the birth of mature ministries, those who would arm their churches for war.

The faultfinders and gossips are already planted in the church – perhaps you are such a one! When the living God is making your pastor more deeply dependent, and thus more easily shaped for His purposes, do you criticize his apparent lack of anointing? Although he did not abandon you during your time of need, do you abandon him now when your faith might be the very encouragement he needs to fully yield to the cross?

Those who are sympathetic to the accuser of the brethren fulfill, by application, Matthew 24:28: "Wherever the corpse is, there the vultures will gather." The backbiting of these vulture-like individuals actually feeds their lower nature, for they seek what is dead in a church; they are attracted to what is dying.

Eventually these faultfinders depart, instinctively looking to take issue with some other church. "These are grumblers, finding fault ... the ones who cause divisions" (Jude 1:16–19). They leave behind former brethren severely wounded and in strife and a pastor greatly disheartened. Soon they join a new church, and in time God begins to deal with this new pastor. Once again the faultfinder spirit manifests itself through them, strategically positioned to destroy another church.

Today God is seeking to raise up His servants with increased power and authority. In the pruning stage of their growth, will we water their dryness with prayer and encouragement, or will we be vultures drawn to devour their dying flesh?

HOW TO CORRECT ERROR

When the accuser comes, it brings distorted facts and condemnation. Those who are manipulated by this spirit never research the virtues in the organization or person they are attacking. With the same zeal that the faultfinders seek to unearth sin, they ought to also seek to know God's love for those they condemn.

True correction, therefore, will proceed with reverence, not revenge. Indeed, are not those whom we seek to correct Christ's servants? Are they not His possession? Is it possible the works of which we are jealous, and thus critical, might be the very works of Christ? Also, let us ask ourselves: Why has God chosen us to bring His rebuke? Are we walking in Christ's pattern?

These are important questions, for to be anointed with Christ's authority to rebuke, we must be committed to men with Christ's goal to redeem. But if we are angry, embittered or jealous toward another, we cannot even pray correctly for that person, much less reprove him. Jesus, the great Lion of Judah, was declared worthy to bring forth judgment by virtue of His nature: He was a Lamb slain for men's sin. *If we are not determined to die for men, we have no right to judge them.*

If you feel unrest and believe it is time to leave and join another church, openly communicate your intentions with the ministerial team. If you are leaving because of issues in the church, my opinion is you should let the leaders know your thoughts. Your comments, spoken in love and humility, may help them better respond to the needs of the church. If you are uncomfortable speaking directly to them or if you are leaving because there is flagrant, serious sin in the leadership, you may want to compose a note. Again, speak with humility but state your case and pray for them in a supportive and sincere way (without self-righteousness). While it is not always possible, those leaving one church to attend another should aim to accomplish that transition in an honorable and loving manner.

Additionally, local ministers should be in communication with one another, never basing their opinion of another church or leader on the testimony of one who has just left it. If people join your congregation and bring with them a root of bitterness against their former assembly, that root will spring up in your church and many will be defiled. Therefore, no matter how much you need new members, be cautious about building your congregation with individuals who are bitter or unreconciled to their former fellowship.

Indeed, the Lord's word to us is that in the house of the Lord criticism must be replaced with prayer and faultfinding eliminated with a covering love. Where there is error, we must go with a motive to restore. Where there are wrong doctrines, let us maintain a gentle spirit as we seek to correct those in opposition.

Lord Jesus, forgive us for our lack of prayer and the weakness of our love. Master, we want to be like You, that when we see a need, instead of criticizing, we lay down our lives for it. Lord, deliver Your church of this demonic faultfinding spirit! In Jesus' name. Amen.

—Adapted from *When the Many Are One*

15

An Unguarded Heart

I know a few will regard the following remarks as coming from "the deep end." Others will take what I'm presenting and exaggerate it beyond its legitimate boundaries. But I want to focus on one reason why some leaders have serious moral failures. I want to offer an insight into how all of us, as Christians, can protect ourselves from a similar failure.

The idea that a leader whom we've known and loved should suddenly be exposed in a devastating scandal seems incomprehensible. Certainly these who have taught others could teach themselves. Is there not resident within them saving knowledge that would protect them from worldly passions?

What is it then that can worm into an individual's thought-life, burrow into his heart, and then grow so compelling that a leader is willing to risk everything he's loved and attained for a mere fulfillment of the flesh? Is it just sin? Or is there something deeper – a lack of spiritual discernment – that left the heart of that leader vulnerable to demonic manipulation?

Their heart was unguarded to the exploitation of hell.

An Unparalleled Warfare

Please note that I am not blaming the devil for every sin we commit. The fact is, selfishness and self-indulgence, which produce sin, are basic instincts of our fallen nature. At the same time, let us also discern the unique warfare of our times. Our world has been flooded with hyper-sexuality and excess. The "red-light district" has moved from the city and entered our homes via the Internet, movies and television. We deceive ourselves if we think we can accommodate an immoral imagination and it not contaminate how we act out our lives.

You see, an unguarded mind that willfully harbors darkness will have spiritual predators cultivating and probing our moral weaknesses. Indeed, through modern technology, an alternate reality – a fantasy world created by our mind's imagination – can be created and accessed by the demonic realm. We don't just watch movies; we are absorbed by them. We actually have sports "fantasy leagues" and computer games and apps that guarantee their programs will be addicting.

There is much within the fallen human nature that can be exploited and plundered for evil. When we do not guard our hearts and avoid what is sinful, this fantasy realm unfolds into darkness, leaving our thought-processes open and unprotected against demons that build strongholds in the human soul.

Listen well: what entertains us actually *enters* us. If you are entertained by pornography or sexual fantasy, perverse or corrupting thoughts, you are opening your soul to hell. You must confront this battle honestly, repent of sin, and set a guard over your heart. If you don't, your battle will advance from temptation to serious, hidden sexual bondage, which in turn will advance to secret attempts to openly fulfill your heightened passions.

People of Destiny, Take Heed

Jesus reveals that a major source of this sexual manipulation is the Jezebel spirit (Rev. 2:20; see chapter 12 in this book). The rampant immorality we see manifested in Western culture underscores the increasing influence of this ruler of darkness. Indeed, compare our world today with cultural standards of just fifty years ago and it's easy to see that Western civilization is under siege. Too many Christians have their defenses down, and many otherwise good people have slipped into bondage.

Yet Jezebel's arsenal includes more than lust; there is also witchcraft, which attacks and works to disarm the conscience. Remember Jehu's words? "What peace, so long as the harlotries of your mother Jezebel and her witchcrafts are so many?" (2 Kings 9:22).

We are fighting the "harlotries" and "witchcrafts" of Jezebel. Those who have been defeated by this spirit often feel they were drugged by their own passions. They did things that were flagrantly sinful, almost daring God (or the devil) to expose them. I am talking about the war against church leaders. How many more must fall before we realize the need for repentance and discernment?

THE SUBTLE ATTACK

The Jezebel spirit is a "man whisperer." Its approach typically is not bold but enticing – seducing and stimulating the degrading thoughts of human flesh. Its quiet power overwhelms and then disarms the human conscience. In your desire to walk upright before the Lord, what you may actually be fighting is Jezebel – in particular, her many "witchcrafts."

One may argue, "My battle is just sin, not warfare." Perhaps that is true for you, but for others it is a spiritual attack on an unguarded heart. Its power may be aimed at Christians in general, but its specific target is church leaders and those called to places of authority in God's kingdom.

There are times when I think the world has greater discernment than the church. Consider these select words from the old Frank Sinatra song, "Witchcraft":

> *Those fingers in my hair*
> *That sly come-hither stare*
> *That strips my conscience bare*
> *It's witchcraft*
> *And I've got no defense for it*
> *The heat is too intense for it*
> *What good would common sense for it do?*
> *'cause it's witchcraft, wicked witchcraft*
> *And although I know it's strictly taboo*
> *When you arouse the need in me*
> *My heart says "Yes, indeed" in me*
> *"Proceed with what you're leading me to"*
>
> —C. Leigh, C. Coleman

The song did, in fact, reveal characteristics about the effect of witchcraft. The composers wrote, "[It] strips my conscience bare." It continues, "I've got no defense for it/The heat is too intense for it/What good would common sense for it do?" And then, "When you arouse the need in me/My heart says, 'Yes, indeed' in me/'Proceed with what you're leading me to.' "

Of course, we do have a defense for it in Christ, but that defense begins with guarding our hearts from the opportunities and deceptions of the Jezebel spirit.

SET A GUARD

I don't want to make too much of the possibility of witchcraft, for becoming overly focused on this type of warfare can itself become a swamp of darkness. Let's keep things in perspective. However, this is a book on discernment, and we need to be aware of the spiritual realm around us. Whether witchcraft is what you are fighting or just natural weaknesses of the flesh, you need to close the door to the hyper-sexuality of our world. Indeed, the world has "no defense for it."

However, for those in the kingdom of God, "the weapons of our warfare are ... divinely powerful" (2 Cor. 10:4). Our weapons and defenses are mighty, but we must use them. Scripture commands: "Watch over your heart with all diligence, for from it flow the springs of life" (Prov. 4:23). The NIV says it this way: "Above all else, *guard* your heart, for everything you do flows from it."

A *guard* is one armed and trained to recognize an enemy and turn away that enemy's attack. We are in war and must stay militant in attitude throughout our lives. We cannot be casual with sin or temptation. When you use the Internet, use a filtering software program as a guard. Be accountable. Don't feed your sexual appetites, for these kinds of addictions only go from bad to worse (Rom. 1:24–28).

If you are currently in bondage to sin, as powerful as the sin seems, the enemy will also work to isolate your battle from others. The efforts we spend hiding sin are the very tools Satan uses to entrap us in it; so, talk to someone (Eph. 5:11–13). If you have a history of sin, then begin a process of cleansing, of washing your "robes ... in the blood of the Lamb" (Rev. 7:14). Confess your sins one by one to God and one another.

Now would be a good time to build yourself up spiritually. Take the next step in your spiritual journey. Get back in the Word, for the sword of the Spirit is the Word of God. Use the authority of God's Word to defend your heart against spiritual attacks.

The most important thing you can do is to return wholeheartedly to God. The Lord promises, "Because he has loved Me, therefore I will deliver him; I will set him securely on high, because he has known My name" (Ps. 91:14).

Beloved, it is time to set a guard over your heart.

Lord God, this day I humble myself before Your throne. You see my heart and the battle I have faced. I ask that You restore me; make me wiser. Let not my enemy triumph over me. Fill me with Your Holy Spirit and grant me the grace to walk with a pure heart, a guarded heart, before You. In Jesus' name. Amen.

16

GOLIATH HAD
A BROTHER

Here's the scene: You are in a battle against sickness, oppression or some similar struggle. You seek God, and in some way the grace of God touches your life. Your victory may have come through a word or prayer or some other encouragement, but you absolutely know the Lord has delivered you. Using the five smooth stones of divine grace, you defeated your Goliath.

But then, a few weeks or months or perhaps years later, all the old symptoms suddenly return with a vengeance. If you were struggling with an illness, it manifests worse than ever; if your battle was regarding a relationship or a particular sin, it seems as though all progress has been lost. You are back to square one.

Have you ever been there? These negative experiences can drain the faith from your heart. You lose the anticipation and power of faith, and a spiritual paralysis immobilizes your soul. You may still attend church, but your faith is unresponsive. When others testify of deliverance, you worry secretly that they, too, will "lose their healing."

For many, the result is one of faith-shaking disillusionment. Scripture says, "Hope deferred makes the heart sick" (Prov. 13:12). This "heartsickness" is a spiritual disease that can cripple your walk with God. Remember, faith is the substance of the things you hope for; if you lose hope, your faith becomes hollow. How can you trust God when it seems as though He let you down? You wonder: *Did I lose my breakthrough, or was I only deceiving myself and never really had it?*

Dear one, it is very possible that what you are experiencing is not a loss of God's blessing but an entirely new spiritual battle. This new war is a very clever and effective deception that Satan uses to try and worm his way back into the lives of those delivered by God.

I had been praying about this very thing, this recurring battle, when the Holy Spirit spoke to my heart: *Goliath had a brother.* I was immediately reminded of David's war against the Philistine giant. We all know that David became a great hero by trusting God and defeating Goliath. However, things changed as we see in 2 Samuel 21:

> *Now when the Philistines were at war again with Israel, David went down and his servants with him; and as they fought against the Philistines, David became weary. Then Ishbi-benob, who was among the descendants of the giant ... intended to kill David. But Abishai the son of Zeruiah helped him, and struck the Philistine and killed him.* —2 Samuel 21:15–17

Years after David conquered Goliath as a lad, after he became king he had to face other giants. In fact, 1 Chronicles 20:5 reveals that at least one of those warring against David was "the brother of Goliath," and four were his children (2 Sam. 21:22). We can imagine that these giants, being Goliath's kin, looked like Goliath, boasted like him, dressed like him and probably even smelled like him. The Scripture says that while fighting one of the descendants of Goliath, "David became weary" (2 Sam. 21:15). The Bible is silent as to what might have been going through the king's mind as he battled these giants. Perhaps he wondered, *I thought I killed Goliath. What is he doing back?* But Goliath had not come back; he was dead! David was actually fighting the giant's kin. *It just looked like the same battle!*

Likewise, you also have had many successful victories. Just because the current giant you are facing looks like one you defeated in the past, do not accept the lie that you never really won the first battle! By the strength of God's grace, you trusted the Almighty and conquered your Goliath. The first giant is dead. Satan is masquerading as your former enemy so he can slip past your shield of faith and thus regain entrance into your life. Resist him. Do not accept the lie that you were never delivered. Stand in faith. Faith is the victory that overcomes the world (1 John 5:4).

The living God who helped you conquer Goliath will empower you to overcome his brother as well.

Father, I come to You as Your servant. Like David, I have become weary with fighting an enemy I thought I had defeated. By the power of Your Holy Spirit, however, I expose the lie that this is the same foe I previously conquered. In Jesus' name, I rebuke the enemy. I ask You, Lord, to send angels to strengthen me supernaturally, just as angels often strengthened Jesus. In the name of the Lord, Amen.

—Adapted from *This Day We Fight!*

17

YOUR APPOINTMENT STILL AWAITS YOU

APPOINTED TIMES

In spite of escalating turmoil in our world, there still remains one last, great outpouring of mercy before the time of the end (Matt. 24:14; Acts 2:17). This supernatural season is not something for which we must beg God. No, its coming has been predetermined. It is the "appointed time" of the Lord.

As most know, an "appointed time" is an open display of the sovereignty and power of God, whether it is in calling a person or calling a nation. In it we discover with absolute certainty that nothing is impossible for God. It is a season when God fulfills the hopes and dreams of His people.

As it is written,

*But You, O Lord, abide forever, and Your name
to all generations. You will arise and have compassion on Zion; for it is time to be gracious to
her, for the appointed time has come.*
                                    —Psalm 102:12–13

During an "appointed time" it is as though the Lord
physically rises and moves in unfailing compassion on
behalf of His people. It is the time when divine promises, dreams and spiritual hopes are fulfilled. Recall:
Abraham and Sarah had waited in faith for a quarter-
century for the promise of God. Finally, as they neared
one hundred years of age, the Lord told Abraham, "At
the appointed time I will return to you ... and Sarah
will have a son" (Gen. 18:14). One year later, "at the
appointed time" (Gen. 21:2), Isaac was born to aged
parents!

While there are, indeed, appointed times of judgment (Mark 13:33), this phrase most frequently represents a time, preset by God, when He invades mankind
with "wonders, plans formed long ago, [that unfold]
with perfect faithfulness" (Isa. 25:1).

Demons may stand arrayed against the Lord; nations may align themselves to fight Him. It does not
matter. "He who sits in the heavens laughs" (Ps. 2:4).
For He makes all things His servants (Ps. 119:91),
even His enemies' plans for evil are reversed and

made to serve the purpose of God (Gen. 50:20; Rom. 8:28; Acts 2:22–24).

If God gave you a vision, a spiritual hope or dream for your future, there will be an appointed time when that which God spoke comes to pass. Thus the Lord assures us, "Record the vision and inscribe it on tablets, that the one who reads it may run. For the vision is yet for the *appointed time*. It hastens toward the goal and it will not fail. Though it tarries, wait for it; for it will certainly come, it will not delay" (Hab. 2:2–3, italics mine). Though your vision may tarry, wait for it. For it will certainly come to pass at the appointed time.

APPOINTED SERVANTS OF GOD

Consider the Lord's word to His disciples. He said,

"You did not choose Me but I chose you, and appointed you that you would go and bear fruit, and that your fruit would remain."
—*John 15:16*

The disciples certainly felt that they had chosen Christ. Yet the deeper truth was that God chose them before the foundation of the world. Likewise, He chose us and predestined us to come to Christ (Eph. 1:3–5). We could not even come to Christ had not the Father drawn us (John 6:44). Yet He who chose us also appointed us to bear fruit. The same power that worked in us our surrender and faith continues to work in our hearts, appointing us to bear fruit. Do you believe God has chosen you? Then believe also that He has appointed you to bear fruit.

THE ENEMY'S WORK

One may argue, "But I know people who were good Christians who have fallen away." Yes, but in most cases you will find that prior to falling away they fell into deep disappointment about a failed spiritual expectation. *Disappointment is not just a sad emotional state of mind; deep disappointment actually can sever our hearts from faith.* It can "*dis*-appoint" us from our appointed destiny.

I have known many who were doing well, moving toward their destiny. The future God had for them seemed close enough to taste. Then they became disappointed in someone or something. By accepting a demonically manipulated disappointment into their spirits, and letting that event germinate and grow into a disappointment with God, a bitter cold winter overtook their souls and their destiny went dormant.

When one is dis-appointed, he is cut off from his appointment with destiny. Their appointed breakthrough remains in the heart of God, but the individual is isolated by unbelief. Hope deferred has made their heart sick. It is here, even in the throes of disappointment, that the righteous must learn to live by faith (see Hab. 2:1–4).

Listen well my friend: *Satan will stop your destiny if you accept the power of disappointment into your life.* Disappointment cuts us off from our vision, and without a vision people perish.

Therefore, let me ask you: Are you carrying disappointment in your heart? Renounce it. Forgive those who have let you down. Have you personally or morally failed? Repent deeply and return to your Redeemer. Right now, I ask the Holy Spirit to remove the paralyzing sting of disappointment from your heart! Holy Spirit, deliver your people this day from the effect of the disappointment. Let them know that their appointment with destiny is still set.

—Adapted from *This Day We Fight!*

18

ONENESS: THE MEASURE OF MATURITY

The most important goal in our lives is to walk in oneness with God Himself. Whether we discuss the attributes of humility, love, faith, worship, etc., the ultimate expression of each of these virtues is to functionalize our oneness with God.

Yet consequential to our oneness with the Lord is our growing oneness with others. That is to say, our unity with Christ also serves as our source of unity with one another, whether those relationships are with other Christians, or in marriage and family relationships, or even with our neighbors, friends and local community. If we apply the standards set before us by Christ, they will lead us into some measure of unity with most others, especially with other Christians. As

Jesus Himself prayed, "I in them and You in Me, that they may be perfected in unity" (John 17:23).

Of course, we may feel the need to be alone at times to recharge and reload; even Jesus did this regularly. Still, the Lord's will is that our lives, gifts and graces fit together into a body, a living organism where the many of us become the one body of Christ. As John's gospel states, Christ came "not for [Israel] only, but in order that He might also gather together into one the children of God who are scattered abroad" (John 11:52). It is the work of the Holy Spirit to gather and unite God's children.

Paul put it this way: We maintain the "unity of the Spirit ... until we all attain to the unity of the faith, and of the knowledge of the Son of God, to a mature man, to the measure of the stature which belongs to the fullness of Christ" (Eph. 4:3, 13).

Note Paul's vision: "We all ... [become] a mature man." The plural becomes singular when the goal is conformity to Christ! When true Christ-centered unity is manifest, the Father adds His endorsement: genuine miracles, transforming power and effective evangelism. Out of unity in the body of Christ comes cultural transformation, the end of which is that "the world [itself] may believe" (John 17:21).

I'm emphasizing this point of unity as a matter of grave importance. Indeed, Paul wrote that many were sick and many, in fact, had died prematurely because they were "not discerning the Lord's body" (1 Cor. 11:29–30 NKJV). The context tells us that they failed to revere the unity of the body and, as a result, their disunity and selfishness restrained the power of Christ's healing. Sickness afflicted the church in Corinth because they failed to discern the Lord's body.

We, on the other hand, too often not only fail to discern and honor different expressions of the local body of Christ, we boast that we are *separated* from other Christians.

Of course, let me emphasize that I am speaking of born-again Christians in our community who attend other fellowships outside of our own. Instead of grieving over our divisions, we have made our separation from others a matter of pride, and even a proof of orthodoxy!

Here again is Paul's warning:

For I am afraid that perhaps when I come I may find you to be not what I wish and may be found by you to be not what you wish; that perhaps there will be strife, jealousy, angry tempers, disputes, slanders, gossip, arrogance, disturbances. —2 Corinthians 12:20

I wonder if Paul is speaking of ancient Corinth or is he talking about us?

You see, to "attain to the unity of the faith" with other Christians is an esteemed place in our spiritual development. Consider also that ever since the eternal words were first uttered, "Let Us make man in Our image" (Gen. 1:26), God has envisioned mankind reflecting His glory through our Christ-centered oneness.

As Jesus Himself prayed,

> *"The glory which You have given Me I have given to them, that they may be one, just as We are one; I in them and You in Me, that they may be perfected in unity."* —John 17:22–23

If we will sincerely pursue walking in the image of God, remember: though He is three persons, it is written, "The Lord our God is one Lord!" (Mark 12:29). This model of three persons, each working in divine and seamless symmetry – a union of nature, of purpose, of unspeakable love and unlimited power – this is the image in the mind of God for man, where the many become one.

You see, the created pattern of "in the image of God" was not only to reflect the reasoning and emotional qualities of God, but in particular the *unity* of the Godhead. Even the phrase, "Let *Us* make," speaks of the plurality within the singularity of the Godhead.

Likewise, the Lord desired to make man as an individual, singular, and yet in functionality, plural: "male and female" (Gen. 1:27). The man named the woman "Eve." God, however, called them both "Adam," for He saw the two as one (Gen. 5:2 KJV).

Thus, when we consider the outworking of the eternal idea – that is, mankind in God's image – its fulfillment manifests most perfectly in the Christ-centered unity of God's people.

19

THE BATTLEGROUND
OF DIVISION

While the work of God is to unite us to Himself and, through Him, to those in relationship with us in the body of Christ, most of us believe that division among born-again Christians is an unfortunate but acceptable reality. This tolerance of fleshly division in the church is a deception and it needs to be discerned as such (1 Cor. 3:3–4). Indeed, to be passive and accepting toward disunity and strife is to cooperate with it, as Jesus warned, "He who does not gather with Me scatters" (Matt. 12:30).

We may not all meet in the same building; we may each be gifted with different graces and talents, but if Christ is dwelling within us then we are His temple. Our unity is essential to the work of God in our region. Knowing this, Satan's strategy is to manipulate all manner of issues, preferences and differences to divide us.

Certainly, it is inevitable among free-will beings that we will have, at times, disagreements. Thus, we must discern the attempts of Satan to manipulate our disagreements to bring division and strife into our midst. Note that I am not speaking of unity with everyone who calls themself a Christian, for not all who call themselves Christians are truly followers of Christ. There are false prophets and charlatans that Jesus warned would deceive even the elect if it were possible. *We must be discerning: some divisions are righteous, even courageous!* For some of us, the Lord may call us out of openly heretical or blatantly compromising churches or denominations.

Yet when Satan steps into the discussion, it is amazing how flimsy some of the issues are that he uses to divide us. He gives a self-righteous air of legitimacy to minor preferences, as though the color of the church carpet was the moral equivalent of someone denying Christ. Again, the real issue isn't about how long the sermon should be or what style of worship we should have or whether we should meet in homes or church buildings – things that mature, humble Christ-followers might easily work out. The real issue is how can we, in spite of differences, humble ourselves while reaching for oneness in Christ?

We must determine that if we divide, it is not because we have been demonically manipulated over minor issues. Therefore, let us ask the Holy Spirit to examine us, especially during times of heightened tensions or strife, and make sure that our motives are free of religious pride and selfish ambition.

In truth, religious pride and selfish ambition are what fueled Lucifer during the great war in Heaven. It is remarkable that at some point prior to the creation of man Heaven itself endured a time of strife. Lucifer challenged the authority and leadership of God. The result? Hell was created. *I want to emphasize this truth: Hell did not exist nor was it part of the creation of God prior to the Great Rebellion. Hell was created to accommodate the unholy demand of Lucifer's ambition. And we, too, create a hell when we are driven by selfish ambition.*

The Bible says, "Where jealousy and selfish ambition exist, there is disorder and every evil thing" (James 3:16). The strife Christians experience today, in a real way, is a continuation of the great primeval conflict, especially when jealousy and selfish ambition creep into a church to divide leadership. Instead of being our brother's keeper, we become a threat, destabilizing the peace and love in the body of Christ.

Lucifer used slander and deceit to seduce angels into rebelling against God. The result was that glorious angels eventually became hardened demons. Likewise, when we open the door to strife and division, our hearts harden. I urge the church to guard their hearts, for if they find they are hardening inside, it is a sure sign the present conflict is being stirred by hell.

ONE WHO DIVIDES

From Heaven's viewpoint, when Lucifer fell he no longer retained the name Lucifer but instead was called "Satan" or the "devil." The meanings of these two names give us discernment into what we are fighting during a division. *Satan* means "one who opposes" or "adversary." When we seek to advance some virtue in the world, there will be an adversary, usually spiritual but often human, who will resist our efforts. When there is strife, there will be a dark power pushing against the efforts of peacemakers to facilitate reconciliation. This resisting power can muscle between those in dissent and those in leadership. All sides must beware. Satan will fiercely oppose the idea of healing and reconciliation.

Let us also look at the name *devil*, which means "slanderer." To slander means more than "to speak evil of one to another." Speaking literally, the word *devil* means "one who puts himself or something between two in order to divide them."

Satan's goal is not just to speak evil; it is to put something between people in order to divide them. This dividing work destroys friendships, marriages and churches. The evil one will exaggerate what seems wrong in one person and twist the remarks of the other person's reaction. He will seek to frustrate our attempts to compromise and will repeatedly divide Christians with new issues.

It is a mark of a church under demonic attack that the criticisms of the divisive group never let up: settle one issue and three more erupt. When Satan manipulates a splinter group within a church, the issues that inflame them cannot actually be satisfied. The pastor's answers do not satisfy nor are attempts to compromise usually effective.

The issues rising between opposing camps are a smoke screen used by Satan to divide and conquer a church. They seem real enough, but when an issue becomes more central to a relationship than humility, love and faith, that issue is really a wedge sent to divide.

You see, the real issue is this: In spite of our differences, will we defend the unity of Christ within the fellowship? Will we leave our offering at the altar and be reconciled with our brothers? The question is, when we find ourselves in times of strife, can we discern the work of the enemy that separates us from our oneness in Christ?

—Adapted from *A House United*

PART THREE

FOLLOW THOSE WHO FOLLOW CHRIST

Redeemer's kin, you too will pay a price.
You will become unoffendable.
Your love will rise to maturity.
And your eyes will fix themselves
upon the possibilities of God,
not the limitations nor frailties of man.

Brethren, join in following my example,
and observe those who walk
according to the pattern you have in us.

— PHILIPPIANS 3:17 —

20

TRUTH IS A PERSON

As we have often stated, our destiny is, first of all, to attain the likeness of Christ. We will fall short along the way; we will have much to learn, relearn and unlearn; we will face many obstacles, but our life vision must not deviate from this goal.

Along the way, there will also be false teachers and ministers. How can we discern the true from the false? In answer to this important question, the Bible itself provides a number of fundamental tests to authenticate the soundness of one's doctrines. One test in particular comes from the apostle Paul. He writes,

Test yourselves to see if you are in the faith; examine yourselves! Or do you not recognize this about yourselves, that Jesus Christ is in you –

unless indeed you fail the test?
    —2 Corinthians 13:5

Paul takes all of Christianity and sums up its entire body of truth into one irreplaceable reality: *"Jesus Christ is in you."* This reality is the one needful thing that Jesus said was necessary. We might be misinformed about the timing of the Rapture or misguided in our administration of church government, but Paul says a true Christian is one who has accepted the living reality of Christ into their hearts!

Do you see this? We are saved, not because we said a prayer at an altar; we are saved because when we prayed the Spirit of Jesus Christ actually entered our life! When He promises, "I will never leave you nor forsake you" (Heb. 13:5 NKJV), He means He is with us forever. The devil knows we are Christians not because we carry a Bible but because we actually carry Christ; Christ's presence is a flame of eternal life within us.

It is Christ dwelling in us that produces fruit, works deliverance, and manifests power through us. Our living union with Him makes us His temple; our connectedness to Him enlivens us as His body. In the swirl of religious deception in our world, all we need to know about truth and error can be found by focusing on Jesus. He said, "I am the way, and the truth, and the life" (John 14:6).

I believe it is vital to have right theology, but truth is more than theology. "Truth," Paul tells us, "is in Jesus" (Eph. 4:21). And when Jesus is in us, He transforms us.

Consider also the profound words Paul wrote to the Galatians:

I have been crucified with Christ; and it is no longer I who live, but Christ lives in me; and the life which I now live in the flesh I live by faith in the Son of God, who loved me and gave Himself up for me. —Galatians 2:20

Paul wrote, "Christ lives in me." The Son of God is not a mere doctrine; He is Emmanuel, "God with us." Eternal life comes from knowing God "and Jesus Christ whom [God has] sent" (John 17:3).

So while there are many important doctrines, all of which are worthy of discussion, our single most important doctrine is that Christ is living within us – speaking, loving, healing and guiding those born of His Spirit. When someone postures himself as a "keeper of the true faith," yet he rejects the reality of Jesus Christ living within us, that person reveals that he is the one walking in deception.

For many deceivers have gone out into the world, those who do not acknowledge Jesus

Christ as coming in the flesh. This is the de-
ceiver and the antichrist.   —2 *John 1:7*

TRUTH

In an era of great confusion, we must see truth as a person: Jesus Christ. Everything we need to know about God, Heaven, hell, salvation, sin, and redemption is centered in Him. We must also apply our hearts in humility and focused faith to become like Him, even as John taught, "The one who says he abides in Him ought himself to walk in the same manner as He walked" (1 John 2:6).

Eternal life does not come from having a religion *about* Christ but from actually *knowing Him* (John 17:3). He has purchased our forgiveness, our healing, and our well-being. As our Redeemer, He works all things for our good. As our King, He grants us His authority and sends us as His ambassadors. He calls us His body, underscoring His oneness with us. And He extends to us His sanctification and righteousness. We are His bride, wooed by His love.

If anyone tries to convince you that Christ does not dwell within His people, remind them of His Word: "If anyone loves Me, he will keep My word; and My Father will love him, and We will come to him and make Our abode with him" (John 14:23).

Beloved, truth springs from our oneness with Jesus Christ. Our vision is nothing less than "Christ in [us], the hope of glory" (Col. 1:27). Warn those who pick at peripheral doctrines yet deny the indwelling of Jesus Christ: The test of true faith is "Jesus Christ ... in [us]" (2 Cor. 13:5). Yes, remind them that truth is a person, not merely a doctrine.

21

PROPHETIC PASSIONS AND PROTOCOLS

When I came to Christ in 1970, America was already pre-wired with end-of-the-world forebodings. Nuclear war seemed inevitable, as Barry McGuire's dire hit "Eve of Destruction" warned. Revolution and lawlessness were spreading everywhere. Yes, the "times" were certainly "a-changin'" as Bob Dylan sang, and indeed so were we. From the rapture-ready hippie revival in the Jesus movement to Hal Lindsey's culture-shaping book, *The Late Great Planet Earth*, the charismatic movement emerged on the world scene overstocked with prophetic anticipations.

Thus, our preoccupation with all things prophetic has been a kind of spiritual birthmark; it is a prominent characteristic of who we are as last days

Christians. Indeed, the '70s produced at least eight major end-of-the-world warnings from prominent authors and various church groups. Other warnings came in the 1980s, punctuated by the book, *88 Reasons Why the Rapture Will Be in 1988.* In the 1990s, especially with the approach of the year 2000 and the widespread computer failures expected from the Y2K Millennium bug, still more warnings came.

I do not doubt the sincerity of anyone who sounded the alarm prematurely. To me there is a difference between a false prophet and a wrong prophet. Yet when will we honestly look at this issue? False alarms have repeatedly misrepresented the Lord's coming over the last forty years.

On the front end of these apocalyptic warnings, evangelists report significant benefits: increased participation in altar calls and certainly more prayer and repentance among Christians who respond. Yet when the pre-announced date passes uneventfully, the effect of being wrongly warned leaves many hearts hardened and cynical.

Meanwhile, the nonbelieving world observes the self-induced anxieties spilling from the evangelical world. In response, they fortify themselves against a religion that, to them, has symptoms of mental illness.

WE CAN DO BETTER

Certainly the Lord has an upgrade for our current version of prophetic ministry. I am not talking about diminishing our fear of God or losing sight of our very prophetic times, but there are biblical procedures that need to be followed – guidelines that would increase prophetic accuracy and thus bring more glory to God.

First, in defense of prophetic ministries, let's remember that it was God who placed prophets in the church (1 Cor. 14). The power released by a humble, accurate, new covenant prophet can be a revelation of the Lord Himself, causing people to fall on their faces in worship (v. 25). I have often been encouraged and guided by a prophetic word. Confirmed prophetic words, as Paul wrote Timothy, are spiritual weapons. They help us "fight the good fight" (1 Tim. 1:18).

Yet there are boundaries. Writing as "a wise master builder" (1 Cor. 3:10), Paul counseled, "Let two or three prophets speak, and let the others judge" (1 Cor. 14:29 NKJV). The admonition to minister as "two or three" instead of as a singular individual is an important safeguard. First, it tells us that no matter how spiritual we consider ourselves, we do not see the whole picture; we need others. Jesus sent His disciples out in twos. He also spoke of the power that is released when two or three disciples gathered in His name. The Revelation of John tells us that the last great prophetic move will be heralded by two prophets (not one) speaking and ministering together (Rev. 11).

Paul again repeats the principle of two or three in his second letter to the Corinthians, saying, "By the mouth of two or three witnesses every word [Gr: rhema] shall be established" (2 Cor. 13:1 NKJV). It is important to note that when it comes to discerning an actual word from the Lord, typically the best a prophet has is a witness of an unseen reality; he does not have a completed "word from the Lord." I know that statement might cause some to react, but let's be honest: there are times when prophets just miss it. By downgrading the weightiness of our communication to a "witness" instead of an irrefutable "word from God," we can avoid serious problems in the future. We give the Lord time to confirm our words supernaturally, perhaps through another ministry at a different time.

Are you a prophet? Instead of saying, "Thus sayeth the Lord," it would be wiser and probably more true to say, "I have a witness for you. Let the Lord confirm it." If you are being ministered to by a prophet and have any question about what is being said, give the Holy Spirit time to confirm His word through one or two more people (unless you have an immediate confirmation in your spirit that the word is God's).

What if you have a national ministry and believe you have a warning to issue? There may be exceptions to this, but I'd suggest you speak it first privately to your peers, as well as to the church leaders in the geographic region where the warning applies. Let someone outside your local ministry team confirm it independently. Give God time to arrange a supernatural presentation of His will. The combination of words that have been confirmed supernaturally by prophetic leaders from different ministries is a powerful catalyst for faith.

The restraints I suggest are not to hamper the prophetic but to place prophets as background players on a stage where the Word of God is the main attraction. One prophet may have a genuine warning yet miss completely the timing of his insight; another ministry knows something will happen on a certain date but isn't sure of the details. Remember, when Paul urges us to "let the prophets speak," he also counseled, "and let the other judge" (1 Cor. 14:29 KVJ). Do not be afraid to let your witness be judged, and if you question a prophetic witness, don't be shy about humbly saying that you don't bear witness.

Additionally, the witness of the prophetic should be measured against the truth of Scripture and also the voice and motive of the Holy Spirit. The prophetic ministry is not a law unto itself but is presented as a humble, yet powerful, revelation of Christ – one that is accountable to church authority.

If you have felt manipulated or wounded by false prophetic words, whether concerning the Lord's return or an imminent disaster or a personal word you were given, I pray you will not lose faith or become cynical. I urge you to heed Paul's words: "Do not despise prophetic utterances. But examine everything carefully; hold fast to that which is good" (1 Thess. 5:20–21).

Remember also that just as we have had certain problems administering prophecy, so there were also problems in the first century. We are not unique. Thus, I ask you to forgive those of us in the prophetic movement who, in our attempt to serve the Lord, may have misrepresented the will and timing of God. Yes, there is a prophetic mess at times, but there are also blessings, as God's Word affirms: "Where no oxen are, the trough is clean; but much increase comes by the strength of an ox" (Prov. 14:4 NKJV). Let's pray for a new prophetic anointing to fall.

22

TRUE MINISTRY
REVEALS CHRIST

A leader will never be perfect, but if he or she loves humility and seeks God in prayer, if they consider themselves spiritually reborn and their primary goal is to be conformed to the life and teachings of Jesus Christ, such a ministry is a gift from God to a congregation.

Each of the ministries mentioned in the New Testament exists for one primary purpose: to reveal the character, motivation and spiritual gifts of Jesus Christ. Yes, they then train and equip others in ministry, but the ultimate goal of God is to functionalize the nature of Christ through a diverse, many-membered body. As Paul wrote, "For even as the body is one and yet has many members, and all the members of the body, though they are many, are one body, so also is Christ" (1 Cor. 12:12).

The Father's plan to create man in "the image of God," as stated in His original purpose in Genesis 1:26–27, is through the indwelling of Christ in the church. As John wrote, "Of His fullness we have all received, and grace upon grace" (John 1:16). When Jesus says we will be able to discern the true from the false by their fruit, He is speaking precisely of seeing the fruit of His living presence manifest through us. If we know Him, we will know those who say they represent Him by their fruits (Matt. 7:15–20). For He is the source of our fruitfulness.

When we submit to the ministry of the pastor, we are not looking to the man but to the love and compassion of Christ, the Good Shepherd, working through that pastor. When we see the evangelist's passion for the unsaved, we are actually looking at Christ's heart. For He has come to seek and save the lost. Again, whether we are encouraged by the insight of the teacher or brought to deliverance by the prophet, in the variety of ministries we are looking to discern the Spirit of Jesus Christ manifest.

Each of these ministries is an extension and expression of Christ. The Lord reveals Himself to the minister's heart with a certain emphasis, then works the uniqueness of His life into His servant.

Thus, we read,

There are differences of ministries, but the same Lord. —*1 Corinthians 12:5 NKJV*

To the degree that all of us, different as we are, flow together in love, honor and unity, to that measure Christ is revealed to the world through the church. Where there might be differences in the church, and these differences might cause division, our oneness in Christ showcases the life of His kingdom, which is a culture of harmony, power and love.

Of course, no one is perfect or complete yet. We are looking to discern the treasure hidden in the field. A pastor or teacher may be imperfect in many ways. But his goal should be apparent: He is seeking daily to become more like Christ.

Prior to when I first came to Christ, I had been part of the hippy culture, living in Berkeley, California, and then Hawaii. During those years I adopted many of the beliefs of the far left. When I became a Christian in 1969, I still carried many of those perspectives. In fact, the first church I attended with any regularity was a church that consisted of about twenty hippies and surfers. The pastor of this church was a 65-year-old man whose view of life could not have been more opposite from mine: he was an active member of the John Birch Society, a far right group. This church was his first attempt at ministry, and he was always making statements that seemed contradictory to my view of life.

Almost daily I would ask my wife, "What are we doing with this man as our pastor?" Yet because there were so many young people just like us, we continued attending. I was very critical of Pastor Ed. He couldn't preach; he stumbled daily with his words, and he rarely prayed. Yet week by week I could see him changing. At first he'd boast that he prayed fifteen minutes each day. My wife and I looked at each other and thought, "Fifteen minutes?" We took fifteen minutes to bless our food! The next week he mentioned that he was up to a half hour a day in prayer; the week after that he said he was spending an hour a day before the Lord.

Around that time Denise and I moved onto their church campus, but we rarely saw Pastor Ed, for he would leave in the morning with his dog, Jennifer, and spend the day in the woods and fields across the street from the church. Though we didn't see him, we did hear him: he spent hours upon hours alone, singing songs to God and praying loudly.

I don't think such changes in your pastor should be patterned exactly after old Brother Ed's, but you should notice a pattern, a conversation or teachings that affirm to you that your pastor or leader's heart is seeking God.

You see, it is not hard to recognize one who has spent an extended time at a newsstand: his conversation overflows with the drama of current affairs. It is also not hard to discern when a person has been to a sporting event, as their expression reveals the outcome of the game. Likewise, people can tell when an individual has spent time seeking God. An imperturbable calm guards their heart, and their countenance is radiant with light. The leaders we need must be people who, though flawed, spend time with God. It should be clear that their goal is to be conformed to Jesus Christ.

I am not saying theology or doctrinal matters are unimportant. God forbid! No, but there is something that transcends right knowledge, and that is a right heart. Paul said, "Follow my example, as I follow the example of Christ" (1 Cor. 11:1 NIV). In discerning who will be your minister, look for the revelation of Christ in that leader's life.

ADDITIONAL THOUGHTS AND INSIGHTS

(Topics too short to make full chapters
but too important to leave out)

JUDGMENT: THE PERFECTION OF LOVE

First, I need to make it clear that I do not see Christ as One without anger. There are evil things in our world that are actually "detestable in the sight of God" (Luke 16:15), and Jesus abhorred them. He was obviously grieved concerning the callousness, pride and lack of compassion in the Pharisees and scribes of His day (see Matt. 23). He also reproved His disciples for their jealousy and selfish ambition (Matt. 20:20–28). And He rebuked the masses for their unbelief, complacency and failure to discern the times (Matt. 11:21; Luke 19:44). Worst of all would be the anger Jesus felt toward someone who caused "little ones who believe in [Him] to stumble" (Matt. 18:6).

If we desire to be like Christ, we must remember these attributes as well. Indeed, these passions, along with the times Jesus wept (Luke 19:41; John 11:35), reveal a very human side to our Lord. If we are alive to the heart of God, we will certainly have times when we are outraged by sin in this world.

Yet the Gospels repeatedly reveal that the great majority of Christ's life was given in love for mankind. From healing the sick to driving out demons to laying down His life for men, His heart was compelled by love, even to His dying prayer: *"Father, forgive them"* (Luke 23:34). Jesus did not let His outrage minimize His capacity to love. He is the Good Shepherd. And even while people slandered Him, His attitude was always, "Whoever speaks a word against the Son of Man, it shall be forgiven him" (Matt. 12:32).

What we see in Jesus Christ is the perfection of love, not judgment. Actually, the perfection of love *is* the perfection of judgment. And while we too will have brief moments of righteous anger, let us remember the Lord's admonition: let him who is without sin cast the first stone (John 8:7).

The Supreme Value in Knowing God's Word

At various places in this book I've mentioned that our foundation for discernment comes from studying God's Word. Over the years I have read through and studied about thirty different translations from start to finish. Reading different versions is an excellent way to view the various shades of meaning in the truth of God.

Someone might think it is a great task to read the whole Bible through, but it only takes studying four chapters a day to read the Bible in a year. We should stay faithful with daily reading, stockpiling the truths and information, and categorizing truth we've gleaned in our studies. I would encourage everyone to be a student of the Word, to memorize Scripture and let God's truth be your truth.

In my study I divided the Bible into sections: the Pentateuch (the first five books of the Bible), the kings, the wisdom books, the prophets, the Gospels, and finally the rest of the New Testament. I would read one chapter from any four of these sections of the Bible. When I completed a section, I would move on to another section. This kept my interest level high with the variety of truths presented in each grouping.

However, if the Holy Spirit began to reveal some theme or insight, I would follow that train of thought to wherever it took me. Also, I'd often put several Bibles at the foot of my bed, kneel with a notebook and pen, and study various translations and renderings as I went.

If you are a disciple, you must accept a more disciplined, mature approach to study. Some Christians never get beyond the book of Leviticus, but if you read Hebrews at the same time, it is remarkable how wonderful our salvation will appear.

The most important revelation you can have when reading the Word, and especially the Gospels, is the realization that you're not just studying doctrine or rules; you are gazing upon God Himself. The Scriptures become a window through which you can actually see God. When I find myself face-to-face with the chaos of my fleshly nature, I do not hide my darkness from the Lord. Rather, I thrust myself, darkness and all, into the fire of His creative love and abilities. I know that what He will do in me is not unlike what He did with the pre-creation universe.

An Encouragement to

Police, Judges and Military

It was mentioned to me that there are some whose livelihood and calling positions them in situations where they must judge other people. And it is true that people in law enforcement especially are required to judge. Yet I think if we consider these occupations, we can develop perspective on the whole realm of judging.

For instance, police are actually trained to look for clues, listen for hints and discern other indicators that lead them to arrest people they suspect are criminals. Unless they actually see a crime being committed, they must also consider those they arrest as "innocent until proven guilty." Then, typically, a court consisting of a judge and jury see the evidence that's presented, hear testimonies of witnesses, and listen to the defense attorney and the prosecutor before rendering a verdict. It is a lengthy process.

We, on the other hand, criticize people as though we are the arresting officer, judge and jury – and all in a matter of moments we declare people guilty. And we assume we are right to do so. This is certainly a problem!

Concerning people in law enforcement, yes, they are called to judge. But wouldn't it be even more powerful if they added to their arsenal of investigative tactics the ability to hear from the Lord? They might sense where a criminal was hiding or which car had drugs, etc. As a policeman, how much more effective would a person be if he or she had spiritual discernment to help guide their natural discernment?

HOW TO DISCERN WITCHCRAFT
COMING AGAINST YOU

Experiencing the effects of witchcraft might not be a common occurrence for most, but it may be something that targets a church leader. The symptoms are as follows: Witchcraft will cause confusion. You'll lose track of your spiritual vision and feel mentally weakened, even physically clumsy. Witchcraft will also stimulate unreasonable fear and engender strife between you and others.

Of course, there are natural sources for all these symptoms as well, but the ones I mentioned are what typically accompany witchcraft.

While there are actually people who seek to use occult or demonic powers against the church, the main source for witchcraft is not what comes from non-Christians but what comes through the mouths of gossiping, negative church members. Let me give you an example: Let's say a fellow named John backslides over a weekend. He gets drunk, spends his paycheck on binge drinking, and is gone all night from home. By Sunday morning he recovers enough to want forgiveness, so he decides to go to church. At the same time, many people have heard of John's sin, three of whom are sitting in a room at church talking negatively about him. One says, "I always knew John was a sinner"; another chimes in, "If I were his wife, I would divorce him," and so the conversation goes. Suddenly, the door opens and it's John. Immediately shame covers everyone in the room; all eyes drop to the floor as a deathly pall manifests in the room. That "deathly pall" is witchcraft. It is a witch's craft that's not being practiced by non-Christians, but by Christians who do not discern the power of their words.

John leaves the room, but he is wiped out. He felt the weight of darkness. He had come to church to get his life right with God, but now the depression that drove him to drink has taken hold of his mind. He's confused, weak, and sick to his stomach. Looking for a place to be alone, he enters another room at church where there are three people who have been trained spiritually; when they see a need, it is a call to pray, not judge. They too are communicating, but with God.

"Lord, forgive John, we pray. Raise him up to be a warrior for You!" says one. Another pleads, "Oh, God, empower John with virtue, with spiritual strength and victory; strengthen his wife as well." And on they pray. John walks into this room and they rejoice that, first, John came to church and then that the very man they were praying for is standing before them. John feels the weight of witchcraft leave as the power of redemption sweeps into his soul.

If you have been a target of negativity or gossip, Jesus gave a clear path to victory. He said, "I say to you, love your enemies and pray for those who persecute you, so that you may be sons of your Father who is in heaven" (Matt. 5:44–45). In essence, you must make the negativity of others become an opportunity to become Christlike.

A Better Way

A man might be a nominal Christian, mostly unaffected by spiritual things, until one day he reads the Bible and the Holy Spirit ignites in him a fire. If that person remains steadfast in his inspiration, he will increasingly pattern his life after Jesus Christ – that is, he will become more loving, more forgiving, and more ready to give his life for the redemption of others. Spiritual power will accompany his life as he becomes more and more like Christ. As Jesus said, "The works that I do, he will do also" (John 14:12).

However, if a nominal Muslim begins to read a Koran, if he continues his daily reading and feels an increasing zeal toward obeying the precepts of Mohammed, as he continues on, this man will ultimately desire to possess true Islam – that is, total submission to Allah. Among this group, a smaller percentage will fully embrace not only the teachings of Mohammed but his works as well; the works Mohammed did, the follower will also do. The zealot will become militant in his community. He will seek to convert unbelievers by any means, including terror, and if one converts from Islam to Christianity, he will seek that person's imprisonment or death. If one carries this version of complete Islam in his or her soul but does not openly use violence, they will at least sympathize with those who do.

Thus, the radicalization of at least some Muslims is inevitable, for the normal growth of an unrestrained, religious zealot will eventually conform him to the founder of his religion. This means that as long as there are people reading the Koran, there will be a small percentage who will feel justified to use violence to spread Islam. We who live in the predominantly non-Muslim world will have to cope with the violence of these "true believers."

It also means that moderate Muslims must realize that unless they desire war with their non-Muslim neighbors, they will have to expose and denounce the radicalized Muslim, especially in communities where Muslims and non-Muslims live together.

Are you Muslim? Do you want the radical extremist to represent you and your people? If not, then you must find ways to direct the radical Muslim into a spiritual jihad against the sins of his soul rather than a violent jihad against the people of a community.

Are you Christian? You must guard against pre-judging all Muslims, for many people turned to Islam as a reaction to the sinfulness of the West. In a real way, they were seeking God but the church failed them. In this present atmosphere, however, they now doubt the choice they made to follow Islam. Therefore, we must reveal Christ and the love He has for all people if we hope to win Muslims.

And finally, as Christians, we must forgive and pray for Muslims. My wife and I pray daily for Muslims, that the Lord of the harvest would send laborers into the Muslim world and that Jesus would be revealed to them, including the most radical – even those who are prepared to kill non-Muslims.

The radical Islamist will only be won by the radical Christ follower. We must show them a better way.

FRANGIPANE BOOKS

RELATIONSHIP WITH CHRIST

LIKE A WATERED GARDEN is a collection of over 300 quotes, insights, and revelations – nuggets of inspiration and truth – hand-picked from Francis' teachings. We pray this journal will become a companion to those who love the Lord and are in pursuit of Christ's likeness. Ebook version includes pages of beautiful photography.

HOLINESS, TRUTH AND THE PRESENCE OF GOD. A penetrating study of the human heart and how God prepares it for His glory. *Published by Charisma House.*

THE SHELTER OF THE MOST HIGH. Trustworthy, biblical evidence shows that in the midst of all our uncertainties/fears, God provides an available shelter to shield us. Finding this place, nothing we encounter can defeat us. Expanded version of *The Stronghold of God. Published by Charisma House.*

THE POWER OF ONE CHRISTLIKE LIFE. The prayer of a Christlike intercessor is the most powerful force in the universe, delaying God's wrath until He pours out His mercy.

I WILL BE FOUND BY YOU. If we genuinely, from our heart, pursue the Lord, He promises He will meet us. Francis calls the church to a focused season of seeking God. We must have more of God, and God we shall find! *Published by Passio (div of Charisma House Book Group).*

UNITY

A House United. Few works of the enemy are as destructive to the body of Christ as a church split. A wedge driven into the heart of a congregation results in bitterness, grief, and hatred where love once lived. Expanded version of *It's Time to End Church Splits. Published by Chosen Books.*

WHEN THE MANY ARE ONE. How the Christian community – driven by grace, unified in love, and activated by prayer – can bring revival and change. This is a revised and expanded version of *The House of the Lord. Published by Charisma House.*

PROPHETIC/SPIRITUAL WARFARE

THE DAYS OF HIS PRESENCE. As the day of the Lord draws near, though darkness covers the earth, the out-raying of Christ's presence shall arise and appear upon His people! *Published by Charisma House.*

THE THREE BATTLEGROUNDS. *Revised Edition:* An in-depth view of three arenas of spiritual warfare: the mind, the church and the heavenly places.

THE POWER OF COVENANT PRAYER. Gain victory over the effect of curses. Persevering prayer is a must for anyone serious about attaining Christlikeness. Then there is a teaching on spiritual protection. Powerful insights on the nature of curses and walking in spiritual victory/freedom. (Formerly titled *The Divine Antidote*). *Published by Charisma House.*

THIS DAY WE FIGHT! We cannot be passive and win the war for our souls. Francis exposes the disarming that occurs when we accept a passive spirit into our thoughts – it seems innocent, yet it causes us to stop seeking God, ultimately rendering us defenseless against spiritual attack and the weaknesses of our flesh. Essential reading for the overcoming church. *Published by Chosen Books.*

SPIRITUAL DISCERNMENT AND THE MIND OF CHRIST. In a world where hearts harden quickly with every new outrage that emerges in society – where the love of many is growing cold, Pastor Francis unveils the glory of possessing the mind of Christ. This book will open the door not only to sense the Lord's presence but to actually hear His heart and gain discernment from His perspective.

TO ORDER MINISTRY RESOURCES: www.ArrowBookstore.com
FOR TEACHINGS/CONFERENCES: www.Frangipane.org

In Christ's Image Training (ICIT)

Online Correspondence Course

Curriculum developed by Francis Frangipane

In Christ's Image Training offers four opportunities for enrollment in Level I training each year: January, April, July and September.

LEVEL I: Certification offers four foundational tracks: Christlikeness, Humility, Prayer and Unity. Completion time is six months.

LEVEL II: Growing in Christ offers further online teaching by Pastor Francis and other national church leaders. Completion time is three months.

LEVEL III: Facilitation and commissioning provide spiritual equipping for those preparing for ministerial opportunities.

ON-SITE Impartation/Focused Training: A 3-day seminar which can be taken by attendance or CD/DVD albums or MP3/MP4 downloads.

AVAILABLE IN SPANISH!
Contact us at spanish@inchristsimage.org.

FOR ENROLLMENT/MATERIALS: www.ICITC.org

Basic Training Manuals

In Christ's Image Training (ICIT) study series pulls together four key areas of the ICIT ministry: Christlikeness, Humility, Prayer and Unity. Perfect for leadership teams, prayer groups, Bible studies and individuals who are seeking to possess a more Christlike life. It is strongly recommended that these four manuals be read in sequence, as each study is built upon the truths found in the preceding manuals.